HOW TO HOLD ON TO YOUR GUY CARD

(IN A **chick's** WORLD)

About the Author

B.J. Bradley is the author of several books including Henry VIII-Man or Myth, one of the most feared, yet brilliant men who ever lived. The author is married with three children and has worked with many boys from kindergarten to high school as a teacher.

HOW TO HOLD ON TO YOUR GUY CARD

(IN A **chick's** WORLD)

B.J. BRADLEY

For the Giles Street Gang:

Mike Bradley, Dave Brommel, Bob McElderry, Matt McKenney, Glenn Peterson, Scott Peterson, Rich Robbins, Doug Ruschill, and Jeff Smith. Always the men. Always the gentlemen.

-B.J. Bradley

Printed in the United States of America

Winding Road Publishers
April 2016
ISBN 978-0-6152-1989-9 (Paperbook)
Second Edition

Six-year-old Steven had just finished watching the last installment of the "Lord of the Rings" trilogy. He had in depth knowledge of the names of the important characters in the story and could pronounce each name correctly. He understood the movie revolved around a mission and that Sam and Frodo were on that mission. Frodo was trying to keep a ring from the bad guy. He accurately described how Gollum had once been a man and now he was a hideous monster because of greed.

The movie revolved around good and evil. There were numerous battles in the movie, sometimes revolving around grotesque figures. Steven didn't particularly like the monstrous walking trees (trees don't walk, after all), but he could deal with the other warriors except for the giant spider. "Too creepy," he said. The kindergartner understood the men, aka hobbits, in the movie had a purpose, a mission, and that their job was to see it to the end. The pint-sized package described the plot of the story in diminutive detail and understood from a male's perspective what the story was about. No amount of feminism, politics, or media will ever erase who the male is and what he stands for. Men are the protectors, the defenders, and the heroes even if he is a hobbit named Frodo.

TABLE OF CONTENTS

Other books by B.J. Bradley

Henry VIII- Man or Myth

Elizabeth I- Drama Queen

Richard III- The Black Legend

Helicoptering and other Annoying Habits of the Gen X Parent

"To put the world right in order, we must first put the nation in order; to put the nation in order, we must first put the family in order; to put the family in order, we must first cultivate our personal life; we must first set our hearts right".

-Confucius

Section I

Meaning of Man

CHAPTER 1

SEAL OF APPROVAL

In an episode of *The Wonder Years*, Kevin catches his gym teacher playing Santa at the mall. At school Mr. Cutlip is Mr. Macho and if anyone finds out that he is playing the kind- hearted old elf, it could be the ruin of his reputation as the tough PE teacher. Kevin promises the coach he won't say anything, but he lets it out anyway and before he can stop it, a mob of bloodthirsty hormone- ridden boys show up at the local shopping center to catch Mr. Cutlip in his jolly red suit. They are trying to "de-guy" and publicly emasculate him purely for the joy of going in for the kill, but luckily, for the coach, the boys decide they don't want to "bring Santa down". Apparently, it's okay to play St. Nick and still maintain your masculinity.

One fellow summed it accurately when he said, "there are no rules on how to be a man today. Do you remember a point at which you became a man? Maybe you remember something more subtle like being invited into the men's circle to drink a beer with them or maybe a man asked your opinion about something because you had learned a skill that had value. You might be technically literate, or great at fixing cars, able to do body work, or you work as a plumber or electrician and have valuable knowledge. Pivotal points to manhood might be accomplishing a feat: climbing a mountain, winning a champion-ship, scoring a knockout, or pinning an "unbeatable" opponent. Men respect others who have, as Napoleon Dynamite so desperately wants, "skills".

At some point Mom will have to let go of her boy. A boy arrives at a moment when he no longer wants to be mom's buddy or little guy. He wants to be like Dad. He wants Dad's attention. Mom is always good for a hug. Nobody loves you like your mom, but Dad is the person who will turn you into a man. While Mom may be the parent whose presence fills the home most often it's Dad the boy looks to. Whether Dad realizes it or not his son absorbs everything he does. Emasculated men are mama's boys. No normal healthy woman wants to be in com-petition with her husband's or boyfriend's mother.

The art of masculinity (there is an art to becoming a man) has been passed down by men to their sons for thousands of years. In primitive societies, rituals and "rites of passage" were used to bring a boy through childhood and adolescence into manhood. Sons and dads lived close together. Fathers taught their son a trade or skill or bonded through fishing and hunting with their sons.

A rite of passage signals the beginning of a new chapter in a guy's life. People's lives are like books with every chapter being a new phase in life. While some "books" are far more dramatic and exciting than others (being a sports star, a Holly-wood producer, famous scientist, or world-renowned con-ductor) these men all had to pass through adolescence just like anyone else.

Our lives are a series of journeys. Being born, going to school, surviving adolescence and high school, moving away from home, getting married, having children, and loosing siblings or parents. And all the in-between stuff : falling in love, falling out of love, changing jobs or finding one's life's work, parenting children and teenagers, (there's a journey that needs its own book) and the death of a beloved person or pet.

Marks of passage such as graduation from high school or college, joining a fraternity, enlisting in the military, finding the babe of your dreams and marrying her, or bringing a bundle and puddle of joy into the world are all significant points in one's life. All these moves change us in ways. New journeys present new circumstances, which in turn promote new ideas and new ways of thinking. Where is the point at which a boy becomes a man? At twelve, thirteen, sixteen, eighteen?

Jails are full of teenagers who have embarked on their own special "journeys" in the attempt to become men through criminal activities. An adolescent, especially a male, needs confirmation that he is a man. Baggy pants, black fingernails, blue-streaked hair are forms of rebellion as well as risk-taking behaviors such as drinking and experimenting with drugs, or stealing a burrito at the corner convenience store. While not all teens engage in such activities, many dangerous behaviors that adolescent males undertake are to prove they are men. Racing cars, fighting contests in bars (black eyes and scars are a badge of honor), college drinking contests, and taking dares are probably attempts at self-initiating.

At one time, a man knew when he became a man by passing through elaborate ceremonies and by the confirmation of older men that he had "passed the test". Boys need a blessing to mark their passage into adulthood. With so many boys raised in fatherless homes today, for some, the gang has become the "father". Sons need fathers in their lives; dads who will love them, teach them, and discipline them. Jobs sacrifice the life of many men. Success in the work world does not cancel failure at home.

For every 100 girls born there are 106 boys born which is a figure that appears to be a global number. Could there be a biological reason for this? Throughout life, there is a slightly greater mortality rate for males. More newborn boys than girls die prematurely. Boys and young men also engage in more dangerous activities than girls do. High impact sports, auto racing, football, and the majority of the military is comprised of men, and more males take chances. Teenage boys have a higher death rate than teenage girls. In a high school recently, there have been several deaths. None of them girls. There are boys who have died from cancer, leukemia, heart attack, suicide, and one who was playing chicken; driving down a dirt road full speed with his head lights off. The tree won.

Women know they are women. Girls know they are girls. Several life events mark the feminine passage. However, it is different for a boy. When does he become a man? Are men born or made? Does reaching a certain age denote the beginning of adulthood? We all know "men" at age 25, 35, or 45 years old who are still "boys". Today children are maturing younger than ever, yet young men are still living at home at 25 and 30 years old. Healthy grown men do not live at home.

Puberty marks the end of the "little boy". Boys just don't become men, they *learn* how to be a man. A son learns by observation. By what you do, not what you say. He absorbs his father's values by witnessing action, behavior, and attitude. Fathers cannot be involved in their son's life if they are invisible; sleeping in the EZ chair or hiding at the office, zoning out in front of a football game or remarried and living out of state. On the road all week or out on the golf course all weekend does not make Dad available. Many dads are not home a lot. There are those who work 50, 60, 70 hours a week or maybe they travel all week. Was your dad like a visitor in your home?

Are boys more aggressive because they have been taught to be or because they just are? Is the difference between male and females learned rather than biological? Boys are far more likely to be diagnosed with ADHD. The detention room in high school is more likely to be holding a room full of boys than girls. The main obstacle is to get boys to sit still, be quite, and pay attention all day. That's not the way a boy is wired, and not the way a boy learns. That is why 90 percent of adolescents who get in trouble at school are male.

Trying to get a young boy to park it like a statue all day is like trying to keep a pig out of the mud. Little girls delight in telling on Mike, Sam, or Cody because he is not in his seat and not doing his work. While it's easy for precious little Patty to sit pleasantly in her seat, boys learn by doing. Many times school is a snooze fest. Let's face it, it's dull. The teacher is in front of the room, "Wa wa blah, blah, page 43, do 1-24". Fields trips are looked forward to by children with great excitement for a reason. There is a trip involved. On the bus, off the bus. Food involved. Sack lunch or lunch there. A new activity to participate in. It requires involvement and participation. You are learning by doing. Busy not bored.

Did you know that adolescent males are 4 times more likely than females to commit suicide? The majority of juvenile mental patients nationwide are male. The majority of adolescent alcoholics and drug addicts are male. Most crimes are committed by young men. Ninety one percent of violent crimes are committed by males. Boys are falling increasingly farther behind girls in academic achievement.

Today's youth is engulfed in technology: computers, cell phones, BlackBerries, iPods, iPads, and video games. A boy, who at one time, worked long hours on the farm, has been replaced by the suburban kid who lives in the city and hangs out at the mall. With the introduction of machines and computers, brute strength is no longer needed in certain jobs. At one time boys worked alongside dad. Now boys live in suburbia where they hole up in their bedrooms pushing buttons on keyboards and video games.

With the onset of a new century, men left the fields to work in the city. Women demanded equal rights. The role of men suddenly had a big question mark above it. With Dad safely tucked away in his cubicle, Mother became the primary parent and the 1960's idea of what a man is was under way. Unfortunately, boys and men today are "de-guyed" on a regular basis by a philosophy that has existed since the time of the "feminist" ideal of what it is to be a man; that there really is no difference between men and women. Give me a break. Give men a break.

What is missing in our society today is clear cut rituals which mark the end of childhood and designate the beginning of manhood. Boys want to be challenged. They want to earn the right to enter the world of men. Once crossed over the line into the adult male world, a boy is now viewed with respect and has earned the privileges of manhood. Men need a mission or cause. Boys want to be challenged. They *want* to be challenged. They don't want it given to them. They want to EARN it. Youth look to their elders for guidance, for their place in the world. A boy needs: "a vision for manhood, a code of conduct, initiation or ritual to manhood, confirmation of passing the "test", and acceptance by the adult male group".

Currently the law defines age 18 as an adult. At 18, you can sign important documents on your own without obtaining permission from a parent or guardian. Eighteen-year-olds can marry, adopt children, and have an abortion, but can't drink a beer. They can sign a contract, operate a business, and vote for the President of the United States, but can't drink a beer. An 18-year-old can own and drive a car, fly an airplane, hunt wildlife with a gun, join the military, but can't drink a beer. He can buy and smoke cigarettes, serve on a jury, or be imprisoned, and OWN a bar, but can't drink a beer. An 18-year-old can give legal consent for nookie and be the mayor of a city! But he can't_____.Fill in the blank.

Did you know that in the United States of America, there are three 18-year-olds who have either served or are serving as mayor of their prospective cities? Sam Juhl from Roland, Iowa, ended his term January 2010. Michael Sessions of Hillsdale, Michigan went on to Hillsdale College after his term was over. Christopher Seeley of Linesville, Pennsylvania was reelected to a second 4 year term in November 2009. You can run a city government, but … yes, you are correct.

It is essential for a man to feel allegiance to his community, his state, his family, and his church. Men are the leaders and protectors. They are the defenders. They are the founding fathers. They are the writers of the Constitution and the Declaration of Independence.

What makes the military so attractive to a youth is that it is a male-bonding, purpose-orientated testing of a man's endurance and strength. Does he have the right stuff? The military provides purpose and goals with all members working together for a common purpose. Men with purpose. Men with

---

direction. Men on the move leads to responsible men and in turn a healthier man. A man who feels connected to his family feels connected to his community. He is more likely to be occupying a seat on the school board than a bunk in jail. He is more likely to be a Boy Scout leader than a disappearing dad. He is more likely to own a business than suing a business over a spilled cup of java.

Wouldn't it be convenient for little guys to come with a code book filled with instructions on how to be a man with bullet points that marked the transition: puberty, license, first car/first girlfriend/ marriage/ kids/ ect....Boys are a bundle of energy. Just ask any mother. Mothers quickly find out that dealing with little Jeffrey is not the same as dealing with Ava the Angel. Any school teacher can attest to the fact that a classroom can get quickly out of hand when the boys outnumber the girls. Girls provide a calmness to the classroom.

Where does a boy today find his masculine identity? When does a boy leave his mother? He needs a well-defined in-itiation, a test. He needs "a category of rituals that mark the passage of a person through the life cycle, from one stage to another over time, from one role or social position to another, integrating the human and cultural experience with biological destiny: birth, reproduction, and death". When there are no clear-cut rules or points in life to signify the end of childhood, when does a boy become a man? Does he stay a boy? What happens to those men who are still children? They look for a woman who will mommy them. They are irresponsible out of work - I won't just take any job- boys who spend their days playing.

A man has his home and does not live off society. He does not go from woman to woman because he is a man. He does not father children he will not provide for because he is a man. He's not addicted to drugs and alcohol because he is a man. He's not living off the government or blaming society for his lack of skills in finding a job. It is a benefit to society to have raised men, not boys. "Boys" are self-destructive. Boys are children. Boys are not men. Even big ones.

Wouldn't it be satisfying to know that you had made it? You had passed the test. You were a man? We need men to train men to become men. Who will stand up and be a man and do a man's job if society keeps insisting that men and women are not different? We *are* different. Let's not forget that. The sports world is a place where men can be men, but is a man defined by wearing a numbered uniform and carrying a brown ellipsoid down a well-manicured sea of grass? Can being a member of a sports team replace a true initiation, a defined line, into the world of manhood? What about the boys who do not participate in athletics? Are they not men also?

Boys crave the attention of their father. Yet fathers are away at the office, on the golf course, out of town, at a meeting, in the bar or at the gym, in front of the TV or hiding in the garage. The great baseball legend Mickey Mantle had fond memories of his dad who died from cancer at the age of thirty-nine. "No boy ever loved his father more," Mickey said. Mantle once commented that one of the great heartaches of his life was that he never told his father he loved him. Jim Valvano, one time basketball coach at North Carolina State University, once said, "My father gave me the greatest gift anyone could give another person, he believed in me. Be a dreamer. If you don't know how to dream, you're dead." Jim died of cancer at age 47. BE A DREAMER. In the movie the *Man in the Iron Mask,* D'Artagnan is stabbed to death by his own son, Louis XIV. "All I ever wanted to be was him," utters fellow musketeer Lt. Andre dismayed to see his mentor and hero come to such an end. Do you have someone you admire? Someone you respect? Wouldn't it be great if every young boy had a mentor? Someone to guide you through your life's journey?

The Hero's Journey is based on Joseph Campbell's writings. It is about a hero's rite of passage or his initiation into a new world. Many popular stories are based on the hero's journey which is why so many people enjoy them. A good story, a worthy cause, a charismatic character, some heroism thrown into the mix, and you have a man's adventure. The Lord of the Rings trilogy gross is in the billions worldwide.

There are several stages to the journey. Our hero leaves his world, his home, and forges into the unknown. He then goes through a transformation where the old ways of being are replaced by new ways of thinking, which in turn, leads to a new kind of freedom or skill. After having gone through the initiation, he goes back to his beginning destination wiser, more confident, having accomplished or learned something about himself so that he may share his new expertise of leadership.

Hero's Journey
1. Separation (leaving your home)
2. The Call
3. The Threshold (with guardians, helpers, and mentors)
4. Initiation and Transformation
5. The Challenge
6. The Abyss
7. The Transformation
8. The Revelation
9. The Atonement
10. The Return (to the known world)
11. The Return (with a Gift)

Why do all indigenous societies and communities place so much emphasis on Rites of Passage? It has been recognized that the stages of life often meant great changes in the psyche or the hormones of the individual and the marking of these points of change was with a ritual or ceremony in order to facilitate this. Western Society has no clearly defined "becoming a man" ceremonies, man rules, or man rites of passage to signify the end of childhood; instead we have 34 year olds still living at home. We need a hero's journey.

The initiation of boys into adulthood has been performed throughout the world. It was and is recognized that the future of the community depends upon having healthy men as opposed to overgrown boys. The shift from boy to man was seen as being so important that young males were removed from the rest of the community and taken away only to return when they were on the path to manhood. Initiation might include such unpleasant things as tattooing, piercing, or giving scars. Some routes were less painful. Sometimes initiation was psychological: fasting, trials of pain, and seclusion. Passing initiation meant you now held adult privileges.

On an episode of *Everybody loves Raymond,* Ray has gotten into a conflict with a female scout leader over where to set up his "cookie table". He sets his table next to her "spot"; he's not going to let her push him around. The scout leader won't budge or give in to him. In the end, Ray's wife punches the scout leader to defend her man over the coveted "spot". While it plays out very funny, she has in essence "de-guyed" her own husband. Nonsense! No man would allow his wife to deck another woman to protect his honor. Nor would he strike the lady himself. Modern culture has placed women in very masculine roles as defenders of their husbands, crime fighters, and superheroes. I don't know about the rest of the population, but if I'm stuck at the top of a building while flames shoot out of the window, I don't want a woman dragging me out of the burning building, I want a fire*man* to carry me down those stairs!

A great scene in the movie *Wild Hogs* has the real bikers sizing up the weekend warriors and correctly guessing what each of the "posers" really does. In essence, they are accusing the suburban saps of not being "real men". Do you ever feel like you are bluffing your way through life and that you will be found out? That you are not a "real man?"

People are still fascinated by medieval knights and their code of chivalry. These were men doing men things to win the favor of a special female. Knights were athletic and highly accomplished individuals who were not only outstanding athletes, but gentleman as well. Men of honor lived and died by a code. They did not run from a challenge. They stood their ground. The knight was the epitome of manhood; strong, brave, and athletic.

Knighthood embodied a well-defined set of ideals which a man adhered to. Being a knight was the equivalent to living by a special code: loyalty to the king and loyalty to their queen, loyalty to their lord and to their God. "Live pure; speak true, right wrong, follow the king". They saw themselves as "knights in Christ". Knighthood was the personification of manhood; a man of integrity who stood his ground. Chivalry is the combination of qualities that was expected of a medieval knight: courage, generosity, protecting a ladie's honor, and her person. The definition of a gentleman can be traced back to the knight and its code. He is not double minded or easily swayed. He cannot be corrupted. Knights also adhered to the code of modesty. The US Army sports team is still called the "Black Knights".

Entrance into the masculine world of knighthood began as a boy of 7 or 8-years-old. He was sent to the neighboring castle where he was trained as a page and taught the skills of weaponry. The boy was usually the son of a knight or a member of the aristocracy. He spent most of his time strengthening his body, wrestling, and riding horses and learned how to fight with a spear and sword. The young page would practice against a wooden dummy called a quintain which was a heavy sack or dummy with the form of a human. He was also schooled in courtesy, religion, reading, and good manners as well as proper court etiquette by the women of the house.

Between the ages of 14 to 16, he became a squire. His duty was to attend and serve as an apprentice to a knight, which included taking care of his horse and cleaning his armor. Like a caddy to a professional golfer, the adolescent followed his knight serving, watching, learning, and competing in tournaments. From his mentor he learned riding and all the skills of war, as well as hunting, hawking, and other sports. By now, he was ready to learn the real duty of a knight. The young man would practice holding his sword which could weigh as much as forty pounds.

Age 18 to 21 marked his initiation into knighthood. The young knight would kneel before his lord who would tap him on each shoulder. He was now a knight. His duty was to "protect the weak, defenseless, helpless, and fight for the general welfare of all".

The knight's code. It was a good idea in theory, but very few people can live up to such stellar standards. Nevertheless, the code of a knight left no room for doubt as to how he should conduct himself. Although knights followed a strict code, tournament play was different. Tournaments were "mock warfare" to impress the ladies as well as the crowd. The joust was considered a "war game". It was practice for the real thing. Just like in a modern tennis match, umpires stood by to make sure knights followed the rules. No cheating. Winning was for one's reputation. Galloping wildly towards one's opponent was dangerous whether you meant him harm. Knocking your rival from his horse was the goal. Jousting was very popular. Man against man. Each knight thundering on horseback across the field to knock his opponent off his horse. His weapon was dulled so as not to hurt his adversary, but opponents were sometimes hurt or even killed as is the case of Henry VIII who was a superb athlete and famed jouster. He was seriously hurt in a tournament. Some say that the many bumps and falls that he took in his youth resulted in his mental instability in old age.

"No day was a good day unless Henry had practiced his beloved sport. One might find the King charging a practice dummy or playing for real with his favorite companions. Of course, that meant Charles Brandon. Jousting could be a dangerous sport. A close minion of Henry's, Francis Bryan, had lost an eye in the tiltyard. During a tournament in January 1510, two fellows were heartily engaged in a battle of jousting. As the young men turned to leave, one of them was recognized. "God save the King!" yelled a surprised spectator. Henry threw off his disguise to shouts of "Hooray!"

Knights and chivalry have faded out. The notion of a gentlemen defending his personal honor now seems as remote as the days of the swashbuckling pirate on the high seas.

It is the role of the elders to create a rite of passage, an initiation of a boy into manhood because when there is no clear-cut definition of what makes a boy a man, society ends up with big boys. A healthy society needs men.

Our rites of passage connect us to life and from generation to generation. Men are drawn together, to hunt, gather, explore, and conquer. They are here to pass down the history that connects us all together. Stories are the blueprints of human existence. Stories link generations together through common language, common ideas, common history, and common culture. Stories connect us to the human race. At one time they were passed through the elders.

How does one go from being a boy to a man? Through a test, a ceremony. Confirmation. Acknowledgement. The boy has reached the age of maturity and responsibility which leaves no doubt in his mind or the community in which he lives that he had truly passed the test. Rites of passage make men out of boys.

DADS ARE REPLACABLE AT WORK!

DADS ARE NOT REPLACEBLE AT HOME!

A Native American elder once commented: You know a civilization that lacks rites of passage, because it has a sick soul and you know it is sick for three reasons:

1 There are no elders
2 The young are violent
3 The adults are bewildered....

America is sorely lacking in producing healthy, productive males. The United States has 5 % of the world population, yet 25% of the world's incarcerated. What does it say about a society where 1 in 32 adults are in jail or prison, on probation, or on parole ?

CHAPTER 2

TWO SOUPS FOR A CRACKER

The first jail in the United States was built in James City, Virginia in the 17th century. At one time people were punished for crimes by being flogged, forced into hard labor, forfeiting some of their property as restitution to the victim, being placed in the stocks, or hung from the gallows. Today it is incarceration and males make up 93% of the prison population.

Many men who find themselves in jail or prison are uneducated or have no marketable skills. While it is appealing to some to take the first "high paying" job after high school, after a few years down the "Road of Reality", real life starts to set in. The two-dollars-above- minimum-wage salary cannot purchase a decent car, home or apartment to live in, cover all the bills, or treat a woman well. A guy can only go so far layering tomatoes and sliced chicken on a hoagie and that's where the temptation of criminal behavior comes into play. Little money leaves no options. It is easier to deal drugs then to become a pharmacist. It is easier to break into someone's home then to get an education and buy your own. It is easier to rip off someone's car than to make car payments.

If you don't think it will ever happen to you, check out these statistics: There is roughly 750 per 100,000 residents in the

United States who are behind bars. It's a sad fact that men are 10 times more likely than women to end up in jail or prison. All the energy and testosterone bottled up in a 5' 9" package is bound to find inappropriate paths unless it is funneled into something productive: a job, school, or the military. The inmate population is mostly a male problem. As a rule, women don't commit violent crimes. Our prisons and jails are not filled with women.

Two-thirds of all crimes are committed by males under the age of 25; one-half of all crimes by males under 20. (Females committing crimes are outnumbered 7 to 1 by males.) Of all age groups, 15 to 16 –year-old boys are the most likely to commit a crime. Poor Huck Finn would be considered a criminal today with his running away, smoking, and floating down the river to nowhere. You will find the same people are often arrested and re-arrested. Jails are in essence "recycling inmates".

The states with the highest rates of people incarcerated are Louisiana and Georgia, with more than 1 percent of their populations in prison or jail. Rounding out the top five states are Texas, Mississippi, and Oklahoma. The states with the lowest rates are Maine, Minnesota, Rhode Island, Vermont, and New Hampshire. Jails not only hold people who have committed minor offensives, but are also holding tanks for inmates who will be serving time in prison, both state and federal.

Just by observing the way you walk down the street, a police officer can tell a lot about you. His business is to "read" people and he has had plenty of years of experience dealing with people from every socioeconomic class, gender, and age. Your mother has nothing on a cop; he has seen it all, every kind of crime and criminal imaginable. Most people have never experienced this world and probably have no idea what it's all about. It is not television where some great looking blond babe in a short skirt with the IQ of Einstein tells some schlup to put his hands up, arrests him single handedly, hauls him to the "precinct", and solves the crime in an hour while not smudging her lipstick.

Police officers seem to have a sense or intuition about people as well being trained in the technical stuff; knowledge of crime and criminal behavior. No one understands evil more than a cop. He has seen it. He has seen it all. For a seasoned police officer, it probably takes something bizarre or unordinary- if there is such a thing in the criminal world – to catch him by surprise. The most routine traffic stops can lead to intriguing finds: rolling meth making laboratories, a high school student with a gun on school property, or in the case of one stop, a dead body in the back seat waiting to be dumped. Experienced cops call it "reading the street". He is always aware of what is going on around him. Certain things might catch his attention and it is not always how someone looks. As they say, looks can be deceiving, but people carrying gym bags are another thing.

People who know each other personally or as acquaintances commit most murders. Murders are not always glamorous like the "movie of the week" spoiled country club brat who poisons poor old dad because he wants his inheritance early. Sometimes murders are committed over things as trivial as a turkey leg or an ice cream cone. Almost all murders are committed between partners: wife/husband and girlfriend/boyfriend. Most killers are men. The person who "discovers" the body is often the killer. Routine calls can be anything but. The officer never knows what is in store for him. Anyone of any age can pull out a weapon as is the case of a 7-year- old who stabbed a cop.

Interestingly, it is the opposite with those who commit rape. The perpetrators of rape are often strangers, but a child molester is frequently in a position of trust: the school counselor, janitor, Boy Scout leader, youth counselor, or so-called "pillar of the community". They can also be a family member or stepfather, stepbrother or grandfather.

Most burglaries and robberies are committed by drug addicted people who need more drugs. In the case of white collar criminals, investment schemes and embezzling are the chosen crimes. These crimes often get out of control. What starts out as just helping yourself to a little turns into excessive grabbing. Often times the thief needs more and more to offset his gambling addiction, drug addiction, or to keep up with the Jones'.

Prisons hold about two-thirds of all inmates, or 1.4 million and 750,000 are in local jails according to the Bureau of Justice statistics. Prisons and jails added more than 1,000 inmates each week for a year, putting almost 2.2 million people behind bars. Between the years of 1950 and 1986, the jail population tripled. Because of the "war on drugs", prisons and jails are now stuffed with people who have committed drug offenses. Throwing an 18-year-old in jail because he was caught with a joint begs to offer a different solution.

Many people stewing in the tank are waiting for their trial. Judges are hesitant to let loose those who have not been tried, convicted, or found not guilty. While there is no doubt there are probably people sitting in jails who are indeed inno-cent, they have either been denied bond or cannot afford bail and will have to wait for their trial. A lot of people simply cannot afford bail.

Many men sitting in prison are there for selling, using, dealing, or making drugs. The majority of inmates in prison are there because of drugs. By changing how some drug offenses are dealt with, it would be possible to reduce the amount of people who are incarcerated. Mixing people with an addiction to drugs with people who are violent offenders somehow does not seem to make sense. It is one thing to be addicted to cocaine or valium and quite another to have murdered someone.

Interference with official acts, possession of tobacco as a minor, underage drinking, or possessing an open container in your car are all criminal offenses. Giving a false name or infor-mation is considered interfering with official acts. The police do not look too kindly at people who do this. Counterfeiting tickets to a show and selling them to the public, not paying child support, credit card fraud, forgery, drugs, vandalism, running into your girlfriend's new guy's car with a city snow plow, stealing a local news lady's car, tax evasion, starting a riot, breaking court dates, (best to show up for your date) speed chases, 3rd OWI, as well as assault and rape are all crimes.

More men than women have been convicted of violent crimes. Almost all school shootings involve guys and the majority of serial killers are men. The school shootings involve mostly teenage boys and a recent mall and store shooting was done by a young male. There is no such thing as an inmate profile. People who commit crimes come from all backgrounds, ethnicities, and religions.

Court cases involve two types of crime: criminal and civil. Unless there is an actual law on the books that is being violated you cannot be charged with a crime. The internet is an example. There are people who slander others on internet chat sites who are going unpunished. It has become a tangled mess of rumors, slander, falsehoods, and cruelty. Once a negative picture or damaging statement has been posted on the web, whether it is accurate or not, the damage has been done. Laws have not caught up with technology.

Guys are more aggressive than girls. They have up to 8 times more testosterone than females. Hostility leads to violence. We can choose to let the aggression loose and give into violence or we can conquer the impulses. Being a man means learning to control his competitive and aggressive nature.

There are many things the average person can be sent to prison for. Today every inch of a person's life seems to be regulated right down to whether you can smoke on your own farm or spank your own kids. There are millions of pages of federal laws and regulations. There are so many regulations today that it is impossible not to break some of them, even minor ones. Not wearing your seat belt, obeying speeding limits (yeah, we all do that), being in the possession of someone's prescription pills, sitting in a car while someone goes in to make a drug deal, standing next to someone while he is shoplifting; (you were there, could be an accessory)could all get you in trouble.

The criminal process is a degrading process. You will suffer the embarrassment of being arrested if there is probable cause. The officer can arrest you if there is a warrant or if he has personally witnessed the perpetrator in action. Your Miranda rights will be read to you. (You have the right to remain silent…..)You are then taken to the police station where you are charged, fingerprinted, and questioned. You absolutely have the right to remain silent and you should REMAIN SILENT! Cops will make all kinds of promises. They will tell you if you write an apology letter, point the finger at your friends, or say you are sorry, they will be easier on you. THIS IS NOT TRUE. Police are allowed to lie to get confessions. An apology letter is a written confession. Telling on your friend means you are now both in trouble. Saying you're sorry is a verbal confession. The more you talk the more trouble you will be in.

The first thing you will say upon arrest is "I am getting a lawyer". They must stop questioning you at this point. Today, an arrested person may find himself placing his hands on an electronic plate, which scans his fingerprints instead of dipping his fingers onto an ink pad. The prints are then entered into a nationwide database. Your name and the fact that you were arrested will most likely make it into the local paper. It doesn't matter if you are innocent or not. Unless your offense is very minor like trespassing (you may be sent home until your court date) the next day you will see a judge. You'll go back to jail and await your trial or possibly bond out while awaiting your trial.

You may have a jury trial. In order to be found guilty, the case against you will have to be proved "beyond a reasonable doubt". Prosecutors are elected lawyers who control and prosecute criminal cases. If you think you are going to be the guy who beats the system, the Federal government wins 95% of its cases.

Civil cases are different from criminal cases as they involve disputes between two parties who each hire lawyers to represent them to protect their interests.

There are three categories of crimes: misdemeanors, in-fractions, and felonies. Examples of misdemeanors would be trespassing, vandalism, drunk driving, shoplifting, and criminal mischief with varying degrees of seriousness such as second degree or fifth degree criminal mischief. Intent plays a big part in the punishment. Men who commit these crimes will most likely pay a fine or face jail time or both.

Almost everyone has probably had some involvement with an infraction aka your friendly city ordinances. Traffic laws apply here. Breaking these would involve paying a fine: smoking in a public school, not coming to a complete stop at a stop sign, or a teenager talking on his cell phone while driving. (They have passed this in some states.) Felonies consist of serious crimes such as rape, murder, or armed robbery. Homicides are committed by one person against another: vehicular homicide (drunk driver) and self-defense (burglar confronted in one's home). Murder consists of someone who premeditated the crime. They thought about what they were going to do to the victim beforehand and planned it. Once again, intent plays a part in how the criminal will be sentenced.

"Suit and tie crimes" or white-collar crimes are usually committed by educated upper class people. Examples are computer crimes, insider trading, or tax fraud. Embezzling is another such crime committed by people who are usually in positions where they have access to checks, bank accounts, or corporate funds. Computer crimes are unique to our generation. With the advent of "white collar crime" the federal prison camp was born. These people are generally not considered dangerous to society; they are the tax cheats and stock and bond manipulators. (Martha Stewart, Enron)

The first appearance before a judge usually happens quickly; 24 to 48 hours after the arrest and is called the arraignment. You will be dressed in a delightful pumpkin orange jumpsuit, shackled at the wrists and ankles and marched through the court halls for all the world to see. County jails are the worst. They are poorly run, grossly under staffed, overcrowded, lacking in basic human needs and sanitary conditions. When it comes to being transported from the jail, you will be placed in leg irons and handcuffed. If you thought whatever you had done was worth this, read on…

The judge will call your name, inform you of your charges, read you your rights, and set or deny bail depending on the crime. Folks who have committed minor crimes such as a misdemeanor will be fined, given probation, restitution, community service, or committed to a program such as a drug or alcohol "rehab" program. For those arrested for a felony, the accused will enter his plea. If you cannot afford an attorney, you may be appointed a public defender. However, if you are in serious trouble and can afford it, get a competent, well-trusted lawyer whose reputation is well-known in the community. Having a bad attorney represent you is like having your arm severed in a car accident and taking cough drops to fix it. Your injury (crime) should be treated by a competent "surgeon" (lawyer). You do not want a cough drop if you are being accused of a felony. The future of your life is on the line.

There are degrees of crimes and levels such as A,B,C, and D. Your prior criminal history as well as how much of a danger you are to society will figure into the sentencing. The legal system is more concerned about whether it is "mad at you or afraid of you" for committing the crime when sentencing you. Depending on who the judge is, your lawyer is, the state you live in, as well as other factors can determine the sentence. Anyone who has watched the news will notice that people who have committed the same crime are often given different sentences for the crime. Different judge, different state, different defendant.

If found guilty, it is possible that you will spend the next year in jail or years in prison. If you receive any significant length of time maybe twenty or thirty years, the chances of any life waiting for you on the outside won't be there when you are done serving your sentence. Many wives will have divorced and remarried, girlfriends disappeared, children will have grown and moved away, and there will be friends who have died. Currently, with the advances in technology, you will be baffled when you get out. Stop for a moment. Anyone who entered prison in 1988 and got out in 2010 will see a new and confusing world. Since the 70's we have seen desktop PCs, iPads, text messaging, Twitter, the DVD, the CD disk, the SUV, the ATM… things that have totally changed the way people live their lives. You will also enter the world as a convicted felon. Much like the scarlet letter, you will wear this badge for the rest of your life.

Ponder for a moment. Do you really think you are going to get by with it? That you are smarter than everyone else? Modern technology can now place a criminal at the scene of the crime just by tracking cell phone usage. Text messages can be retrieved. GPS can determine where someone was. Learn a trade or skill, get an education; become a chef, a machinist, a dog groomer. Use your gifts. Everyone has them. There is no such thing as easy money. Earn it. Don't steal it. Develop the vision to see the future and the results or outcome of various behaviors like criminal, financial, educational, or familial has on your life. Understanding the consequences of living for what I want now will enable a person to make good choices.

Prosecutors will dismiss the majority of cases which are often too weak to go after. As stated before, if they go after you, they know what they are doing. Remember your kind old Uncle Sam wins 95% of the cases. Prosecutors can pretty much find a crime to fit those they chose to pursue. Many people accused and convicted of crimes are not dangerous, just stupid, greedy, too smart for themselves, ignorant, or were in the wrong place at the wrong time with the wrong people. Many have engaged in victimless crimes. Teenagers get caught up in stupid things: vandalism, criminal mischief, "car hopping" breaking into cars at night and taking CD's or pocket change, assault (fighting some guy they don't like), and harassing their girlfriend. These are crimes and if you are 18 years or older you will be charged. The pain of being involved with the legal system and it is painful, will cure most of those people who get caught up in it. If you end up in jail or prison, be prepared.

The PSR is a presentencing report. It will be like your inmate curriculum vitae. The report contains many things about a defendant such as economic status, job and medical history, family background, whether you have a criminal record, what the current crime is, and details of said crime. It will be the prison's personal guide on how they will view and treat you. You do not want the negative stuff your ex-wife, employer, neighbors, or probation officer has said about you in this report. Anything negative said about you will hound you throughout your entire incarceration. The PSR tells how much time you should serve, what monetary restitution you will owe and comments about your motivation and character. The judge will use the report to help set a sentence. It is always in your favor if you have not been in trouble before and have demonstrated a decent lifestyle.

Officers are trained in the art of lying to get at the truth. He may befriend you and ask for your side of the story. Doesn't make any difference at this point. You are already guilty. He cannot change anything for you. All any more information is going to do is hurt you. You broke the law and they are gonna' "learn you a lesson". You will do as you are told and not ask questions.

There are two ways to get to prison: Self-surrender and to be taken by force. It would be fair to say, that when you are incarcerated, you will not be dealing with a fine educated professional staff. These guys generally have no special training. They are just big and scary. Folks occupying the jail cells can also be a problem. Some inmates are looking for a befuddled scared cellmate who will spill his guts to his new "cellie" only to find the information as they say, "used against him". NEVER talk to anyone in jail. He is NOT your friend.

Since most of us know where murderers and rapists end up, we will focus on the minimum security prison which holds white collar criminals. People who end up in low security prison camps committed crimes without a weapon so they are considered non-violent. A federal criminal camp is like a small village in that everyone knows everyone else's business. Never disclose what you are worth. Prisons are full of con men and people who come from and have nothing. Prison won't change some of the schemers especially if they think you are loaded.

The BOP (Bureau of Prisons) will make sure that you are safe. Dead inmate equals lawsuit and the government does not want that. Inmates are also required to earn their GED before getting out. Currently, the BOP receives about 47,000 dollars a year for each inmate under its control.

You will be a number. The guards will not care what your name is. It is just a job. You are just a number.

If you think jail is free, think again. Prison camps have commissaries where you can purchase many items. You can also choose from a list of items to purchase if you are in a county jail. If you want clean hair and desire personal cleanliness, you will need to purchase shampoo and other personal items. They will not let visitors bring any of these items in. After a man gets out of jail, he will be billed for the days he served which can get rather costly.

You don't want to be caught with contraband or you will find yourself back in the county jail, then onto a more structured environment. Contraband is anything in your possession which you have not purchased in the commissary or you do not have special permission to possess. Contraband is something a visitor or you the inmate have illegally brought in. Not a good idea.

The Inmate Phone System is one of the biggest rip-offs in the United States. They charge outrageous fees from people in tremendous pain. Many inmates do not receive calls because their family and friends cannot afford them. In the beginning, the incarcerated person will be in pain and want to hear a familiar voice on the phone. The phone conversations are monitored and any admission over the phone about anything will be used against the inmate or caller.

Your time with each phone call will last 15 minutes. Many times during the phone conversation, you will hear an operator break in and tell you how many minutes there are left. If 15 minutes is not enough time, you can always call back. You will pay outrageous rates for phone calls at an average of $17.00 per 15-minute call. At 3 calls a day, 7 days a week, it is EASY to spend well over $1000 a month on phone calls. You will not be able to keep racking up calls if you do not pay the bill. They will block your calls and cut you off. There is no such thing as credit with this "phone company".

Many fights break out in the TV room. There is the guy who will monitor what everyone else watches. There are also inmates who will come in and sit in "their seat". Let them have it. You + fight = a higher security prison. Not worth it. Too many written summons means loss of phone and visitor privileges, extra duty, or being confined to the dorm more. Stealing contraband will get you removed from the FPC.

Anyone who ends up as an incarcerated individual should be aware of the "hole"; a holding tank for the man who can't behave himself in prison. It is a solitary confinement cell. If you are really out of control, you will find yourself stripped naked; just you and yourself on the floor of the cell. Fighting with another inmate can land you there. Don't think for a minute your fight with another convict won't be a source of amusement for other inmates or the guards who may themselves try to provoke an altercation.

You will be respectful to the prison personal and other inmates or you will be carted off to the county jail which many feel is worse and then transported to another facility. While many people envision the Federal Prison Camp as some kind high scale incarceration for the wealthy where an inmate works on a tan and plays golf all day, it is not. You are still in prison. A real prison. Any disrespect on your part will be your ticket to a worse place. Your behavior will determine where you end up. Assault and murder are crimes that will send the low security inmate into a high security prison.

Inmates who have served or are serving longer sentences will be jealous of short timers who they think have been clever enough to get away with something because of their money or power. They might try to put you in harm's way just to bring you down. Follow the rules, be civil, keep yourself busy, never talk about other inmates or join in when they are talking about someone else. Your job is to blend into the scenery like a squirrel in a tree. Beware to the inmate who is not liked by the other prisoners (child molesters). He might find all of his things placed on his bed and set on fire. He will be removed immediately. The BOP does not want problems in a minimum security facility. A disliked inmate is a problem.

Diesel Therapy. No, it has nothing to do with fixing up your car. If the inmate is difficult to deal with or just does not fit in, he may be a candidate for this service. The offender is moved from one county jail to another sometimes day after day, sometimes in the dead of the night or early morning hours. They wear the same clothes day after day. Missed meals and missed showers are common. There is also the constant jostling around of prisoners between states and county jails because of "overcrowding". Why inmates are jostled from one county jail to another makes absolutely no sense unless it is to give "therapy" to those folks who cannot behave themselves.

Most FPC's are organized into dormitory units. There are no two alike. At one camp, many meals were served in the original packing trays from Eastern Airlines, a company that filed for bankruptcy protection in 1989. Over 18,000 people lost their jobs and pensions in one day. By 1991, the airline was history. By 2004, their prepackaged food was served at a prison camp.

Many people who find themselves in the FPC will be haunted by their own demons. They are ashamed of themselves and the humiliation they have brought upon their family. Most people are not bad people. They just did something stupid and thought they could get by with it.

There is no such thing as alone time when you are incarcerated. You are always surrounded by people. Curious minds will want know what you did to get into prison. Be pithy and to the point. A sentence or two explanation and no more. Men who are in for the long haul are jealous of those who will not be in prison long. Make it sound like you will be serving the "entire stretch".

High security prisons hold those who have committed serious crimes such as rape, armed robbery, and murder. This is where they belong. Prison also holds the "undesirables".

Prison is full of snitches. High security prison informers usually end up dead. Low security tattle tales are part of the scenery. They are everywhere and their favorite game is to set you up and get you in trouble especially if they know you are close to getting out. Keep to yourself. A secured locker protects you from unwanted contraband. Unfortunately, some of the guards may also try to provoke you into getting into trouble. If you have to, stay put on your cot and read or work on a cross-word puzzle.

Not everyone who ends up in jail or prison is a "criminal" in the sense of what most people think of. Some have made a mistake or error in judgment. They are not career troublemakers who have a rap sheet long enough to wallpaper the bathroom with. That is how the FPC was born; a place to hold white collar criminals..

It would be fair to say that most Americans have no idea what the world of incarceration really is. It is so far removed from normal people's daily lives. It is a world onto its own. If you find yourself in it, it is a total shock not only to the person who has been arrested and incarcerated, but to his family as well.

It is not "reality TV" where the cops chase after some slug while a catchy tune plays in the background. TV tends to glamorize things so that it takes the "reality" out of a situation. It is not clever glib lawyers and investigators who get confessions out of the criminal of the week just in time to wrap up the hour drama. It is not glamorous bounty hunters who tear through town with his trusty family beside him, while actually real, still gives a hint of glamour to a side of life most of us hopefully will never have to deal with. No one ever expects their precious baby boy or husband will end up in jail and many young males do not believe they will actually end up there either.

Anyone who has taken a college psychology course might be familiar with the Stanford prison experiment conducted in 1971. The psychological study exposed what happens to those playing the roles of guard and inmate in a simulated prison and how quickly out of control the experiment became. Led by psychologist Philip Zimbardo, 24 undergraduate paid volunteers were recruited for 15 dollars a day. They were each chosen for their respective roles based on a coin toss. The prison was set up in the basement of the Stanford psychology building.

Within a few days, the guards became surprisingly sadistic (these were nice middle class college boys) and the prisoners had lost their identity and began to see themselves as only a number. No one predicted how quickly the volunteers would adapt to their roles nor how emotionally traumatizing the experiment would be to the "inmates". It took a total of two days for the guards to engage in humiliating behavior towards their charges. The mistreatment was so great that it led the "prisoners" to rebellion and finally the psychological acceptance of their condition. All this happened in less than a week. All of this was make-believe, yet to the young men playing the roles it was real. You can imagine what goes on in a real jail or prison. Except they are real guards and real inmates and the prisoners cannot quit the experiment and go home. The experiment was terminated after six days.

Unless you make a living in the field of law, most citizens have no contact with this world and are not aware of some of the crimes that can land you there. While this is in no way minimizing the seriousness of some crimes and some people should be in jail, Americans have become law puppets.

After you have served your sentence, if you have been convicted of a felony, you are forever a FELON. FELON will be your "Scarlet Letter" that you will carry for the rest of your life. If you are in your twenties, that is a long road ahead. The question is asked on a majority of job applications and you will have to indicate that you are a convicted felon. The word conjures up all kinds images in the average person's mind. None of them good.

Rebellion often leads to a critical point in one's life; the proverbial fork in the road. Am I going to take a direction that will lead me into a life of crime or am I willing to make some changes, accept what life has dropped on me and learn from it? According to Keith Richards of the ancient Rolling Stones, "If you are going to kick authority in the teeth, you might as well use two feet." He has been tried several times on drug related charges and more often than that, had one foot in jail and one in rehab. The rock legend, with his trademark emaciated cadaver image, could easily be the poster boy for what living a hard life and drugs will do to a person.

When harsh life lessons are thrown at us, we become angry and feel sorry for ourselves. Life's lessons are like mosaics. We are only able to see pieces and bits of what has been handed to us when we are deep in crisis. It really doesn't matter how we got there, whether we inflicted it upon ourselves or we experienced it as an innocent bystander. Often after we have lived through the event the parts of the mosaic start to form a picture and we are able to learn from it. Each lesson is filed in your personal mental folder shaping and molding your character. For those convinced they are in control, the only power you really have is maintaining a good reputation which is based on your behavior.

According to Ambrose Gwinnet Bierce, "Law is a machine in which you go in as a pig and come out as a sausage". Amen.

An inmate will be given a "party" when he is being released. These foods can be purchased at the commissary. Hopefully this will be the last time a person is incarcered and the last time he will find himself peddling cigarettes for a candy bar, contact solution for shampoo, and two soups for some crackers.

Inmate Dip

1 pack Ramen noodles
Pop top can of white tuna
1 jar Cheez Whiz
Jalapeno peppers
Saltines or Ritz crackers

There is a total of 2.2 million inmates incarcerated in the United States. The incarceration rate is many times what other countries experience. If you think freedom is your right because you live in America think again. They're building new prisons every day. Ol' Huck would surely find himself in the juvenile system had he been born in modern times.

Laws in the United States of America:

Drinking booze is forbidden at tailgate parties outside sports stadiums in Maryland, but during the game buy booze in the stadium!

In Tempe, Arizona drink booze in a city park if it is no more than three acres.

It is illegal in California for you to possess more than one bear claw.

State law in Arkansas says that you cannot hold office within ten years of fighting a duel or even acting as a second or carrying a challenge. We'll discuss duels in a later chapter.

If someone doesn't accept a challenge to a duel in Michigan, it's a misdemeanor to scoff at him in a poster. The ramifications of not fighting a duel will be discussed later.

Like most states, Arizona forbids dueling. You would also be in violation of a law if you knew of a dueling challenge and don't report it even if the challenge hasn't been sent. (See law above.)

Springfield, Illinois prohibits commercial establishments from permitting or promoting dwarf tossing.

In Vermont, anyone, including a child, possessing a slingshot with the intent of using it can be imprisoned and fined.

In Kansas, if a train runs over you, the railroad company must give your remains a free ticket on the train. Sounds fun.

It is illegal to trespass at night in Oklahoma and injure melons. Whatever that means.

In Carmel, California, men and women must get a permit to walk the streets and sidewalks in high heels. They probably could include other cities in California as well.

Santa Fe, New Mexico at one point was considering a law that would force owners to strap Fido in a seatbelt. (Seriously)

Labeling a high calorie doughnut wrong can get you in trouble. That's what happened to a 68—year-old Illinois man who was sentenced to 15 months in jail for labeling a 530 calorie doughnut low fat.

Paul McCartney and Pete Best, the original drummer of the Beatles, were once arrested in Hamburg for attaching a condom to a nail on the wall and setting it ablaze.

CHAPTER 3

NUMBER 119,104

In the old *Mission Impossible* television show Jim Phelps was given a mission each week if he "decided to accept it". After five seconds, the tape would self-destruct into a vanishing cloud of smoke.

Men accept responsibility when they know the why of what they are being called to do. Responsible men are those who have had role models and mentors who taught the virtues of discipline and responsibility. They have the ability to assume a leadership role when other's lives are depending on them. Self-sacrifice. Mission. Purpose. Albert Einstein once said, "The man who regards his life as meaningless is not merely unhappy but hardly fit for life". A man needs to know that his life has value.

Each man wants to know why do I exist? What am I here for? What are my functions in life? What does God want me to do with my life? A long term purpose is different than a goal, a "goal is something specific you want to accomplish, a purpose is why you want to accomplish it". How does my life, the things I have learned, the things I have experienced, the people I know or have known, and the places I have been fit into my life and what I am here to do. A man needs a clear-cut worldview that fits into his reason for being. Do you really want to feel valuable? Do something for someone else. Are you successful or accomplished in your field? Share your knowledge.

Have you ever noticed how many times we are just a number? You are a 9, 10 or 13 shoe size. The house you occupy is 9204 Smith Street. You are number 62 at the DOT. Number 37 on the basketball team, number 4 on the waiting list at the restaurant, and ring size number 6 ½. We're not Zach, Tom, and Nick, the basketball players. We are number 22, 34, and 18.

We are our battering average .334 and our golf score 76. He is not Seth, Tara's husband. He is Seth second husband, marriage number 2. We are our salary; 32,000, 56,000, or 113,000 thousand dollars a year. We are second chair row d-5 at the concert. In school we were in reading group 1, 2 or 3. In high school we were student ID # 12789. We're 42 long in a sports coat, 15 1/4 in a shirt, 34 waist, 2nd place in hockey, bridge, or water volleyball. It's not the Washington High School baseball team. It's state champs years 2008, 2009. We're 867-2745, boyfriend number 3, fourth child in the family, parking spot 62 at work.

A man wants to be more than a number. He wants an honorable name and excellent reputation. While credit card commercials love to run their "priceless ads", a man's reputation *is* priceless. Anyone who has ever damaged his good name realizes what an asset it is to his family and future. Sometimes the damage is so severe you can never recover your name. A good name means respect from your wife, your children, and your community. A good name means respect for yourself.

A man's values are a reflection of who he truly is, but every man desires to know: What can I give my time, my energy, my life to? Who will I share my life with? The journey is much easier with a partner. Is there a "system" where I can use my talents to benefit others? There are things all human beings need to do. To respect and love their God, to respect and love other human beings, and to take care of and promote their culture and country.

Many moviegoers love to see the hero rush in and rescue his soldiers, his family, his community, or whomever happens to be around when the plane crashes, the ship goes down, the house catches on fire, or the flood waters rush through town.

Men are heroes when the occasion calls for it. They rise to the call. They make a difference. They are able to put their own needs aside for the good of the whole.

Boredom. Everyone seems to be bored these days. Most people suffer too few demands rather than too many. People love "causes" such as the pancake breakfast to drum up donations for a homeless family, a 3 mile walk for the latest "illness" foundation, or the toy drive at Christmas time. While short term causes are good feel quick fixes or "bandages", they are short lived. A burst of purpose-filled days to help others out fill up the "good feelings" tank of the individual temporarily.

Affluence translates into apathy. Today's culture is engulfed in the "What can you do for me?" philosophy. They are in possession of things that people did not have twenty years ago: cell phones, iPods, and personal computers. They do not even have to go to the library today to do a research paper. Instead, they scan the internet, cut and paste, and voila! A term paper. Their lives are devoid of purpose. We no longer have to circle the wagons to keep out the enemy (high tech security systems will take care of that),worry about producing good crops so we survive throughout the winter (that's what the grocery store is for), or bury children who did not survive infancy or childhood because of disease (vaccines before kindergarten).

Many American men today prove themselves through material things. Who has the biggest house, most cars, the most trophies, and best looking babe. Success does not always grant satisfaction. Those surrounded by an overabundance of "trophies" are surprisingly not always the happiest. "Stuff" is poor fuel when it comes to filling the tank of a purposed filled life. Youth offers false immortality. Mid-life offers opportunities that the young are too blind to see. Age offers purpose and mission. It offers fatherhood: being a husband and a member of a family, church, community, and society.

Living in honor is living by your personal code of value, decency, morals. One of the things that keeps many voters from voting for various politicians is their personal life. People don't like guys who cheat while they are married especially when the wife has terminal cancer. There is still a code of honor that people expect their leaders to follow.

The man or "DAD" is now regulated to a cartoon like buffoon on sitcom TV. Mom runs circles around Dad taking care of all emergencies that come up and pointing out all of her husband's flaws. The kids' job is to make Dad the punch line of their jokes because they are smarter than Dad. He's just there to bring home the paycheck so teenage sitcom kids Justin or Jennifer can sneak his credit card out of his pocket to go buy worthless junk at the mall while he lies snoozing and drooling on the couch.

Never ending wants is a vicious circle. It will grab you and pull you under every bit as much abusing alcohol drugs. Stuff is everywhere. The stuff game is one no one ever wins. There is always a newer SUV, a bigger house, a cooler iPad, and a more updated iPhone. By the time you walk in the door and unpack your new laptop it is practically obsolete! The stuff game is a no win game. Buying stuff does not provide a sense of purpose, just more debt.

People often visualize "addiction" as the sallow-faced junkie lying in an abandoned building with a needle hanging out of his arm or a marinated drunk passed out face down in an alley. People don't see addiction as an exercise junkie, compulsive credit card mall shopper, or a one night stand womanizer. Anything done to the point of excess, to the point of hurting one physically or mentally, or financially is an addiction. Is that what you are working for stuff? Stuff? Being addicted to something to the point your whole life is consumed by it is an addiction. Your god is whatever you have to have and today that seems to be junk. Technology makes life easier, provides more leisure time. STOP! I challenge anyone reading this to think about it. Is that really true?

Are you napping and enjoying the breeze at the beach, or on the laptop? Are you mowing the lawn and trimming the hedges to relax or waiting for the cell phone dangling from your belt to ring with a business proposition? Are you enjoying the excellent manicotti at the new Italian restaurant or waiting to hear your name being paged? Are you sleeping at night or tapping the iPhone screen to see who has e-mailed you?

Much of technology has made us into techno slaves. Has the technology in your life raised or lowered your workload? We have literally become "on call" 24 hours a day 7 days week. What if we don't answer the phone, send a text message, or fire off an e-mail? Will you lose your job? The account? Have you noticed how irritated people get when they can't reach you? You don't respond immediately? Does a person have to be at service every waking and resting moment?

Employees no longer have job security because some jobs are being replaced by machines or competitors from other countries. It puts a great strain on people because technology makes your skills obsolete when competing with those young college grads whose skills will soon be no longer state of the art. (Just more updated than yours.) It's sort of like driving a new car out of the parking lot. Once you have that degree in hand and all the things that you learned to get it, the knowledge starts to fade as you stroll off the campus into the world of obsolete technology.

People want it all today and insist on it. When they are unable to achieve the things on their "Everything I need to be happy bucket list" they become depressed. People put far too much value on crap. Humans are not objects. They live and breathe and if they find their lives reduced to a mere existence, they commit suicide. Hence, the unhappiness with mindless, robotic, boring, predictable jobs. To be stuck in one is like having one foot in the tar pit. You are still living and breathing, yet trapped in purgatory. "Despair despite success".

One of the greatest problems facing young adults today is emptiness; rampant drug abuse, apathy towards school, poor relationships, and lack of desire to work all add up to someone who does not seem to have purpose or direction. Are you more afraid of being nothing than of being hurt, poor, or uneducated? What happens when you have achieved significance in the eyes of the world, but not in your own eyes? What matters in life is to achieve something and share it with others. It does not have to be big. No one can hide from the bogeyman or the little "greenman". We will all at one time or another suffer. What direction are you taking? The one to self-pity or the road to meaningful existence? "If you think you can, you can and if you think you can't, you're right".

Are you burned out? If you had to think about it you probably aren't. Times of crisis come in many shapes and sizes. A man is tired at the beginning of the day not just at the end. Long term burnout leaves men drained; emotionally, physically, psychologically, and spiritually. It is not momentary or sudden. It is often a midlife thing. It is also an M generation thing. Pushy parents have prodded their offspring into being sports stars and honor roll students. For years.

Many young adults are burned out by the time they enter college. "Crispies" as college professors refer to them. From the young to those well into their 50's the problem of reality has set in. It's not going to happen like I THOUGHT it would. I am not going to play baseball professionally, get a law degree, own a business, work on a cruise ship, travel to Europe, be my own boss, or run for Congress.

There are many ways to succeed besides having a dynamic career or being a pro ball player. You are only as successful as the way you balance your work and as a friend, brother, son, husband, father, or provider.

Many people equate who they are with their job. When people meet you they want to know what you do. There is a thread of truth that identity is marked by occupation. If what you do is who you are then who are you when you don't do what do anymore? Some men work hard to seek the approval of their own father whether he is still living or not. Chuck Swindoll once said that, "a lie is like a coin, you can spend it any way you want but you can only spend it once". Some men feel like they are living a lie.

A personal calling is found by doing for others. If it is always about you, you will never discover your purpose. The only things we control completely are our character and conduct.

The collective shove of parents today for their children to go to college so they can "get a good job" or worse yet, so they can reap the bragging rights of their young adult becoming a veterinarian, or a lawyer; something they could not themselves achieve. Everyone has gifts that are unique to him. Parents and their children are each unique individuals.

Mr. Beadles was a biology professor in a small college. He knew his subject well. His tests were killers, sometimes going on for pages with as many as 200 questions. Man, it was not as if anyone in the class was going to medical school or anything, but he liked his students, was able to convey a complicated subject so that everyone understood, but most importantly brought the class up to a higher level. The students wanted to do well whether they were interested in the subject or not, because of Mr. Beadles.

Mr. Brewster is a third grade teacher. He has hair the color of golden autumn wheat and is always dressed in a blue shirt and tie. He is kind and fair to the children. Everyone in class is important and he teaches to each child. Third grade was a good year for many of his former students.

Joe manages a bar in a restaurant. He is always out going, cheerful, knows everyone's name and their kid's names, but most importantly he knows what you order whenever you come in! Joe's friendliness translates into a successful business. Joe knows his business, but more importantly, he knows his customers.

Steve works in a body shop. Much to the annoyance of his mother, he started taking anything he could get his hands on apart when he was a little boy. His bedroom always looked like an explosion had taken place. There were bits and parts, screws, and tools smattered all over his floor because he was always in the "middle of a project". When he was a teenager "projects" were moved into the garage. Steve knows cars. You could say he is an expert in his field. People appreciate his knowledge and take their car to Steve when they need repairs.

Patrick began drawing when he was a toddler. He has always had an "eye" for shapes and lines. As he grew older, everyone always knew that he was the "artist" in the class. He sees the world differently than other folks. He is creative and sensitive and does excellent work. Today, he is employed as a graphic designer.

You don't have to be a movie star, a famous athlete, or some genius who works with nanotechnology to be "someone". Even Socrates claimed to know nothing! It is fact that most people are born with average intelligence. Very few people are geniuses, capable of being world-class athletes, or playing the cello with the New York Symphony.

Most people's intelligence falls into the average range.

50% of IQ scores are between 90 and 110
2.5% of people have superior intelligence (over 130)
2.5% of people are mentally challenged (under 70)
0.5% of people are a genius (IQ over 140) (That eliminates most parents' claims that their child is "gifted".)

Over 140 - Indicates you're a genius-. Congratulations!
120 - 140 - Superior intelligence -You're almost there.
110 - 119 – Above average- Just like the rest of us.
90 - 109 – Average intelligence – You' ll be okay
80 - 89 - Dullness
70 - 79 - Borderline deficiency
Below 70 Feeble-mindedness

Today there is more despair about the meaningless of life. We want every need satisfied. We want our life to be meaningful. How much does it take to pay the mortgage, make the car payments, pay for little Chet and Anna's piano lessons, soccer equipment, dance attire, Boy Scout outings or fill your car with enough sound equipment you could broadcast the Cubs baseball game to the block down the street. Do you really need all that junk?

In the autumn of 1942, Viktor Frankl, his wife, parents, and brother were arrested in Vienna and taken to a concentration camp. No longer a respected doctor, he was now prisoner 119,104. While in the camp, his father succumbed to starvation, his mother and brother perished at Auschwitz in 1944, and his wife died at Bergen-Belsen. Only his sister Stella would survive. She was able to escape to Australia. At one point Frankl succumbed to typhoid fever. When Frankl was moved to Auschwitz, parts of a manuscript he had written and hidden in the lining of his jacket had to be thrown out. The desire to complete his work stayed with him throughout his ordeal. He collected bits and snippets of paper so that he could record from memory to his saved scraps what he remembered from his manuscript, "The Doctor and the Soul".

One morning while marching to work in the wretched cold, Frankl was suddenly overcome with the essence of his wife and was comforted by the realization that merely thinking about his beloved companion temporarily transported him to a place of serenity. "The salvation of man is through love and in love". Knowing that he had work to finish and the thought of seeing his wife again kept the cinders of hope lit. Once a person decides there is no hope all is lost. One's meaning according to Viktor Frankl comes through experiential values, creative values, and attitudinal values. Frankl observed that prisoners who had something to look forward to such as being reunited with family, or a work that needed to be finished helped in their survival.

In April of 1945, Frankl's camp was liberated and he returned to Vienna. After his release in April of 1945, Frankl took a teaching job at University of Vienna Medical School. People who could envision the future long enough to survive the present : being reunited with family, finishing work, and those who trusted in God, and had unwavering faith seemed to survive their ordeal. He concluded that the philosopher Friedrich

Nietzsche had it right: "He who has a why to live for can bear almost any how".

Mr. Frankl said, "We who lived in concentration camps can remember the men who walked through the huts comforting others, giving away their last piece of bread. They may have been few in number, but they offer sufficient proof that everything can be taken from a man but one thing: the last of the human freedoms; to choose one's attitude in any given set of circumstances, to choose one's own way."

Why do some people suffer with grace, dignity, and others with anger and resistance? Because those who have found meaning to their suffering are able to endure and live with it. You cannot escape prison, so you have to learn to accept and adapt to it. You cannot grow another leg or arm lost in an accident, so you adapt to the loss by learning to use a prosthetic. One cannot change incurable cancer so he chooses to maintain his joy and sense of humor. And a man cannot change his past no matter what he does. It is done.

Pain is God telling you that something is wrong. Something needs to be changed. Isn't it interesting that momentary pain will often produce a better life. Suffering is not always fair. People suffer for doing wrong, but there are times when we bear the cross for something we do right. We stood our ground and stayed true to our principles. Even more puzzling are times we suffer for no reason. As the byproduct of what someone else has done or circumstances we have no control over. Suffering will make us "bitter or better". Pain has purpose. Pain is the greatest teacher if the student is willing to learn.

"Hope deferred makes a heart sick but desire fulfilled is a tree of life". Hopeless souls are found in wandering shells. No hope breeds ill health, sadness, and anger. Finding meaning to a man's suffering and the things he is dealt, the work he does, the reason he is here heals the heart. Hope is the antibiotic for the sick soul.

Nothing to look forward to. No one to love. Nothing to do. No purpose. No hope. Dead-end job. Getting out of bed every morning requires something to do, someone to love, something to look forward to, and something to laugh about or at least someone to laugh with. Why do you think those late night comedians make the big bucks? We want to end the day on a good note. With a chuckle.

Dr. Frankl knew that looking to the future was man's salvation when life's pain is at its worst. Something to look forward to is something to hope for. Loving someone or having a work to finish will enable a person even in the most dire human existence to propel a man towards the future. Our attitude. It's not what we are dealt with. It is how we respond to it. Each of us is different. Each of us has desires and dreams. And we as humans can withstand anything as long as we believe there is a purpose or meaning to it. For a man to know the "why" for his existence, he will be able to bear almost any "how". We have a purpose, a destination to fulfill. You have a purpose in life.

Viktor Frankl's theory and therapy was based on his years in the Nazi death camps where he was able to observe human beings in the kind of wretched conditions that most people will never experience. It fascinated him how some people were able to survive such degradation while others gave up and died.

A man is able to suffer through the most horrendous of conditions through his ability to receive a higher calling. He who is able to not give into his basic drives, his basic urges, his selfish ego places his energy in finding meaning to his life. No one escapes suffering. As Viktor Frankl stated so eloquently that it is not one's suffering, but the derivation of meaning he takes from his suffering, although suffering does not always give way to meaning. Why else would a person continue to repeat the same mistakes? He has not learned.

A man's meaning in life often comes as a surprise or a byproduct of something obscure, or by accident. It truly is one of the greatest treasures in life: to discover your meaning to learn why you are here.

Viktor Frankl further stated, "Man is pushed by his drives, but pulled by his values." People who are ruled by base level drives seem to have a minimal working value system. How else can it be explained why high profile people give into their basic urges at the risk of losing their family, life's work, and reputation? A man has to have a conscience in order to adhere to a value system.

Meaning is not subjected to freedom. A life has value no matter where the body is: in a hospital, in a prison, in a physically disabled body or mind. One's life can have meaning merely by existing. Anyone, regardless of circumstances, can live his life in a meaningful productive way. Any man regardless of wealth, education, color, and time on earth can carve a meaningful existence out of his life. Men need to be somebody, yet most people spend the precious energy of their lives trying to eliminate risk or squishing it down to a more manageable size. A man needs to be significant, to make a contribution, to have a sense of direction or excitement, to be recognized as an individual of worth and integrity, and to be able to look in the mirror and like what he sees.

According to Sigmund Freud, "The moment one in-quires about the sense or value of life, one is sick."

90% of diseases are stress related.

CHAPTER 4

BABES AND BUDS

By the time a person reaches their mid thirties, there are more women than men. Hence, the many women who keep the television talk show in business complaining that there "aren't any good men left". (Just less of them.) Men don't seem to have in stock an abundance of those infection fighting T-cells which helps fight off disease. Because of this, this leaves men with a weaker immune system. Males are more susceptible to disease including heart, cancer, and stroke as well as being more prone to accidents and injuries.

As people approach the age of fifty, women outnumber men. Many men die before women do leaving an older female population, and most people who reach the age of one hundred are women. Older men probably find themselves for the first time in their life being chased by women only because they have out lived the competition!

Girls are more interested in good qualities than good looks. Hmm. Girls are more interested in good qualities than good looks. Women are drawn to personal character over a pair of square pecs and busting biceps. A woman needs a lover and a warrior not a really "nice guy". Women are attracted to aggressive, strong, powerful males because they need protection, provision, companionship, and a father to help raise children.

Men can possess these attributes without looking like a freak from planet steroid. Also most women do not like "soft" men.

According to rules of etiquette from 1886, "It is the duty of a gentleman to know how to ride, to shoot, to fence, to box, to swim, to row, and to dance. He should be graceful. If attacked by ruffians, a man should be able to defend himself and also to defend women from their insults". It is not the "duty" of man to live off of his woman, his parents, or his government. Chivalry is the combination of qualities expected of a medieval knight: courage, generosity, protecting her honor, and her person. Men not only possess these traits, but should not hesitate to use them. Typically the male conquers and the female nurtures. Women dream of being a princess and being carried off; men being the hero.

Generally, men do not have sweet smelling hair, pressed pants, and matching argyle socks. They do not wear blue and white striped shorts, coordinating shoes with just a hint of baby blue, or have perfectly perfumed coiffed hair. They do not wear perfectly pressed pants nor are they dressed in a shirt so stiff you could eat off of it. There are no ruffles, bows, frills, zigzags, or buttons with cute designs on them on men's clothes. Bleached blond hair? Hmm. For the most part you will not see a man in the fabric store or a gift shop with funny little glass figurines and odd metal sculptures. He is not a Girl Scout leader, school secretary, nursery school teacher, or buffing toenails at the mall while he gives some dainty little gal a pedicure. That's just not the nature of a man.

It is always a red flag when a man does not like animals, does not like his mother or he does not feel the need to protect those who are weak or in need. After all, it is the man who jumps into a raging river to save a stranded person, it is a man who charges head on into enemy fire, it is a man who stayed back on the Titanic, and it is a man who was nailed to the cross.

So what is it with women? What is it with bad boys? How do these two get together? Why do they get together? What would motivate a college educated relatively intelligent woman to fall all over "Mr. Mischievous", the guy who floats between part time jobs, lusts after other women, or has "got an idea", but just hasn't found the "right" people to go in on it with him. Meanwhile, she supports him while he is:

a. In a bar
b. Playing golf
c. Hunting or fishing with the guys
d. Dating woman #2 behind her back
e. Watching TV

No woman is gonna' fix this guy! He doesn't want to be fixed. A real man is NOT that guy. This is what a healthy woman wants, so set your toupee back on the mannequin. A man that:

a. Likes women (Makes life easier for the gal)
b. Likes his mother (BIG SIGN he's not going to hurt his lady and that he will treat her right)
c. Has a job (Always helps, women are not impressed with men who have no job)

About one third of men between 25 and 34 are living at home. One third! P.S. Living at home with parents at age 30; revoke guy card.

The first things we notice about a person when meeting them is skin color, age, sex, height, and the physical size of the person and general overall appearance. You have control over your appearance. Our society stereotypes people based on how they look. It's not fair, but what you wear and how you look says a lot about who you are. Clothes are symbols people base stereotypes on. The way a person dresses says a lot about who they are and how they feel. The latest trend is to wear clothes that do not fit. Baggy clothes. The Goodwell get-up. (Not that there is anything wrong with giving to charity.) But it's tough to look good in clown pants. If you've got something to show, why would anyone want to cover it up under a tent? What impression are you giving out by the way you are dressed?

Cologne should be used to give your body a "signature scent" and should be used sparingly. No one wants to be gasping for air as some guy drowning in a heavy dose of concentrated pheromones passes by.

The beauty of a woman entices a man. What woman does not want a man to find her beautiful? Maybe that is why the regular person finds the "beautiful people" of Hollywood so interesting. He's the epitome of manhood: the square jaw, and the wavy hair. She's the ultimate female: the cascading tresses and the hour glass figure, How lucky can you get! Two gorgeous human beings. Three months later the Hollywood tabloid screams, "Joe Handsome and Greta Gorgeous getting a divorce!" While looks definitely reel in the catch, keeping the mate is a challenge that goes beyond looks.

An attractive woman is often pursued for no other reason than the fact that she looks good. The guy doesn't even know her. Looks don't always equal a great catch, but you never know. A professor at a medical school was aware that a couple of female medical students, one who in particular was very attractive, could not get a date. A doctor? And a beautiful one? Whoa. She simply overwhelmed most men.

Women temper men who are far less likely to have drug or alcohol problems when they are married. Men who are alone tend to have more depression and health problems, higher rates of drug and alcohol abuse, and behavioral dysfunction. Many men do not realize that their wife or girlfriend is their best friend. They do not realize how important she was until they break up, divorce, or she dies.

There better be something beyond those baby blues and long legs. One does not have to be physically beautiful to be a princess. A woman does not have to be stunning to arouse desire. Femininity is far more attractive than a gorgeous woman who "wears the pants". If you are marrying "Barbie" before someone else gets her think about it. Obviously, beauty is not enough. You are marrying the person. If the Princess is so great, why has she been married 3 or 4 times? Any famous actresses come to mind?

Do you know what you are getting into? Do you really want to spend the next 10 years bailing some babe out of debt? Protecting and coming to her aid, while noble indeed, is not your job. A man's job is not to rescue the little woman from herself! While the lure of pulling a woman out of her little ol' mess is certainly appealing to the male ego, in real life damsels in distress are quite another story. It is not your job to pay off her credit cards, make her house payment, pay for piano lessons, or buy groceries. To appreciate what it means to work, *you have to work.* To appreciate earning money from a job, you have to have a job and *earn* money from it. Child support, government support, food stamps, free medical care, alimony, money from a trust or inheritance is not earning money. It is someone else's money: yours – you, the tax payer- and it's not your job to provide a damsel a royal lifestyle on a beer budget.

Nice women will not sleep with you in the middle of divorce or right after the divorce. A decent woman does not leave her children home alone or drop them off at the nearest convenient person's house so she can be with you. Respectable women have good self-esteem, which means an education or good job, and a mind of her own. She does not go along with everything you say or do, has friends that you have actually met, and does not clutch her cell phone in anticipation of your next call.

Many men fall into an affair or get involved with a lover not because they are in love, but because it is an adventure. They have long been told to "be responsible", but the adventurer, warrior, or pirate is still deep in their psyche. Today many men feel like the world is asking of him things he doubts that he has. A doting dame can be a tremendous ego enhancer.

Women don't need a male "best friend". While a woman can have fun and enjoy asexual male company, the basic drive for protection draws women naturally to men, who are well, men! Woman are often attracted to the wild side of men, but once having caught him they begin the job of domesticating their catch. The very thing that attracted her now suddenly needs to be repaired.

Feminism has changed the way women are viewed. Mom no longer runs circles around Dad dressed in her gingham apron while the meatloaf sizzles in the oven. In this day and age, with so many college-educated women who have excellent careers, (doctor, CPA, nurse, regional manager, teacher) she earns her own money and has a mind of her own. If she can make a mean meatloaf after coming home from the classroom, hospital room, or boardroom, consider yourself fortunate. Wouldn't you rather have a partner who is your equal as a human being than a woman who sits by the tower window waiting for her prince to come?

Successful and desirable men come in all sizes. That is why you will see the most stunning women on the arms of average looking medical students, Hollywood agents, and homely sports stars. Nothing sounds quite so good as Dr. and Mrs. So and So... or how about the young women screaming like crazy for the anorexic rock star who looks like a stand up cadaver. Men come in all shapes, but regardless of the size, everything about him says MALE.

According to the current feminist ideal, women are no longer considered "helpless". Well, now, where does that leave you guys? To open or not open the door? That is the question. Your best bet is to treat people with respect. Treat everyone like you would be treated.

What does kindness look like? It looks like a smile. It means being pleasant. Greet people as you pass them. One thing that separates the older generation (besides wearing his underwear on the inside instead of the outside) from the current generation is manners. Step away from the crowd and be the person with good manners. If all else fails and you just don't know what to do, err on the side of good manners. Be nice to both men and women. That way you can't lose. If some radical feminist gets her boxers in a twisted bundle, that's her problem.

You're nice to everyone. The old "respectometer" goes WAY UP when a man opens a door, helps someone push a car out of snowdrift, takes the trash down to the curb, picks the dog up from the vet after "the operation", pumps your gas, and shovels the sidewalk for the elderly neighbor. And don't forget to tell her she did a good job with dinner even if she threw a frozen pizza into the oven. It still took effort to go out and buy the darn pizza and cook it. She made sure that you had something to eat.

If you ask the girl out you should pay for the meal. The host is whoever invites the person out. If you have made different arrangements, that's fine, but buying the meal does not entitle you to anything extra and don't be the kind of guy who pulls the conversation back to yourself. The gentleman's code to treating a woman well is RESPECT. I can hear Aretha singing it now. Make good manners a habit and a part of your daily routine.

Leave the tech stuff off. Many people are glued to their Kindles, laptops, and cell phones. They cannot bear to leave their precious toys even to go on vacation or to church. Have you ever sat in a sermon and someone's cell phone went off? God's calling him? Give me a break. Are you really that important or indispensable that you have to keep the phone ready just in case? Do you really have to answer that call while taking your wife or girlfriend out to dinner? Nothing is more boorish than dropping a live conversation with a real person who is right in front of you to talk into the mouth piece of a mechanical object. All eyes on the subject at hand. Your woman.

Put yourself in the position of a giver of your time, attention, and your friendship. Giving does not necessarily mean showering the lady with a never ending supply of gifts or expensive dinners. Many women just like to know that they matter. Everyone likes to talk about themselves but no one likes to listen to people talk about themselves. Be the listener.

FOR MARRIED GUYS

Parenting is a job for grown-ups. Children need limits.

Oh, they may wail and complain and in the case of teenagers, break some rules, but they still want them. Rules mean you, the parent, care. It is the adult's duty to pass good values and ethical behavior by modeling it. If you want your kids to behave, you have to behave. Even if you are the most responsible human being that ever lived, it does happen that some kids get into trouble or will not follow your lead, and insist upon doing it their own way.

Dad, you cannot be a political leader, be the head of the Shriners, soccer coach, work 60 hours a week and still have enough time to give your children attention. You cannot have it all. Something has to give and it eventually will. The family today is balancing one foot on the beam while the other teeters precariously over the mortgage, second mortgage, the third mortgage, two SUV payments, and the wonderful insurance that goes along with owning pricey automobiles, the kid's activities, credit card debt, and out-of-control teenagers.

The current philosophy is if Dad goes to work, so why shouldn't Mom? Like it's some kind of wonderful adventure that she is missing out of. It's what makes her happy! It fulfills mom. If mom isn't happy no one is. No matter how much the current 21st century person has been bludgeoned into thinking you can have it all, no one can have it all. And the loser of the current philosophy is the guy. Today's mom goes to work, drops clothes off at the dry cleaners, helps kids with homework, cleans the bathroom, volunteers at church and school, drives the little puddins' to camp, soccer, tennis, and band. Anything leftover the cat gets. Dad is like the forgotten puppy scratching at the door for some scraps.

Dad should still be a man when the time calls for a man. Nothing is sadder than a family where Mom runs the show and her partner is only a bit player in the home. We are living in a world today where Dad is the bank, chromosome donor, or both. Who will bring a son into the world of men? Who will safeguard his little daughter? Nothing is more special to a little girl than to be her "daddy's little girl". A daughter needs to know she is valuable; that her dad is a modern day knight ready to defend her honor.

Children really do want boundaries. No matter how loud they scream, no matter how many rules they break, no matter how many classes they fail, no matter how many fender-benders they get into, no matter how many adult beverages they try, no matter how many undesirable friends drop by, no matter how many times they yell, "You're not fair!" You're mean!" (Darn right I am.)

No matter what is thrown at you. Stand your ground. You will not regret it. Never give up. "Right now we are the dumbest people on earth," according to one tired parent of teens. It will pass and one day you will be saying, "Our children don't think we are so dumb after all." At one time Christian values were considered American values. In "the days", teachers were respected conduits for what was taught in the home. A parent knew Junior was going to place his hand over his heart and pledge the allegiance. They knew their little punkin' was going to be taught that Mom and Dad and their little pile of rug rats were the definition of a "family". They knew the little ones were not going to be bombarded with political gunk and ideologies that are both offensive and dangerous. Parents had total confidence the family would be taught their ABC's and three R's: readin' 'rithmatic, and 'riting.

It is important that family values are reinforced at home. If you are fair and have reasonable rules, your grown children will thank you. No job, no house, no new wife, or girlfriend is worth not investing in your children. Nothing you ever do will be more important than raising decent, responsible human beings.

BUDS

Do you have friends who like you because they like *you*. Or do they really like your hot tub, lake cabin, the circle of friends you run with, your position in the community, or your new boat? How many friends do you have that you can stand to spend more than a half an hour with? Who can you can call in the middle of the night when there is an emergency? Who will stick by you when you: get a divorce, declare bankruptcy, lose a job or business, your spouse dies, your child gets in trouble, or gossip stands to ruin your reputation?

Besides being a good time, "hang time" can be comforting (you are not the only one experiencing a crisis), enlightening (maybe a new idea or information was presented), just fun (no one ever died from laughter), and free therapy (just talking about it sometimes gets it out and off your shoulders where you may be able take it on). "Hang time" is people who hang out with you, just because. Some of the best business contacts you will ever make, the best moments you will have with your kids, and the closest moments with your wife or girlfriend will come simply by "just being there".

"A man's man never shows weakness or pain, he is never vulnerable". Most guys try to hold their heavy burdens by themselves. He thinks he can control any situation. When men find themselves in the middle of a divorce, custody battle, lost job, which is traumatic enough for men, they go it alone. Oh, they know plenty of guys: their tennis partner, the guys on the church basketball team, the neighbor whose lawn resembles a checker board, their son's soccer coach, but what about the friend you can call in the middle of the night... Real friends?

A man needs a friend. Maybe that is why the hero and his sidekick movies are so popular. "Starksy and Hutch", Mel Gibson and Danny Glover, and Jackie Chan and Chris Tucker are popular because they embody what it means to be a friend, partner, and the guy who can be trusted to watch your back. The guys are on a mission, they have their trusty partner beside them. Someone they know is not going to jump overboard when things get heated. People love to see real friendship in action even if it is only make-believe on the big screen. Everyone wants at least one good friend.

The women's friendship network is like a giant spider web. Best friends, close family members, good friends, co-workers, special acquaints, sometimes acquaintances, hello acquaintances (the cashier at the grocery store, the dry cleaner, last year's school teacher ect....) When women find themselves in a heartbreaking difficult jam all they have to do is pull out the modern version of a rolodex, their cell phone contact list. Many men find out how "poor" they really are when they lose a job, a home, their reputation, or wife through death or divorce. One is very rich indeed, if he has at least one good friend.

Recently a man who worked for several years at a bank got caught embezzling a half million dollars. He did not turn to friends and family for help. Any normal person in that situation would have panicked, but people will continue to love you even if you have made a mistake. Instead, he chose to murder his wife and four children by bludgeoning them with a baseball bat before dying himself in a blazing inferno after his minivan crashed into a pole off the interstate. Notes he left behind apologized profusely for what he did. The grieving grandparents were left behind wondering. He was a trapped man with probably few or any friends to support him through his ordeal.

Section II

When Men Were Men

CHAPTER 5

RASCALS -THE DAYS OF THE DUELS

C hildren love to hear fairytales and adults love to read "long, long ago once upon a time" stories because men like to rescue and women like to be rescued. In a satisfying fairy tale, the girl gets her man and usually the castle, too. Who can argue with that? Many movies and stories play on the theme of our dashing hero coming in to save the poor princess from her circumstances, her life, her job, her wicked father, her wicked mother, blah, blah, ect.. ect.., but we never get tired of it.

She might be the daughter of a king or common servant but we know she is still a princess. A young girl's boyfriend and his grandparents call her the "Princess" not because she is spoiled and indulged but because she is a likable feminine girl. She is all girl. She is not trying to push herself onto the boys football squad, into a wrestling match, or looking to pull out a cigar and puff her way into the men's board room. She enjoys being a girl and is recognized for it, and yes, she absolutely delights in being called Princess especially in a world where women today are referred to as "hos and bi-ches" in popular music, movies, and in the halls of the high school. That is what boys are being told they are through popular culture. *Jersey Shore* does not exactly enhance the quality of male and female relationships.

A famous rock star was recently arrested and thrown in jail. A customer in a restaurant apparently had "exchanged words" with a lady that was traveling with the star's group which resulted in fisticuffs being exchanged between the men in the parking lot. The star had earlier "decked" another fellow rocker supposedly over a woman. Knight in shining armor? Or jealous guy losing his temper? Defender of a woman's honor? Or drunk pampered star who doesn't like to be annoyed? While knights and chivalry have disappeared into fairytale stories of long ago, the notion of a gentlemen defending his woman has not. While there is no "code" on how to be a man in our current society, men still feel that way.

The following is an overheard conversation:

Boyfriend: "Did you get that new job?"
Girlfriend: "Yeah, I got it and there are a lot of guys that work there."
Boyfriend: "I'm gonna' have to beat off anyone that comes near you."
Girlfriend: Satisfied rolling of her eyes. Her man is going to protect her.
Girlfriend: "When they see those "big guns" (muscles for the politically correct) of yours they'll run!"
Boyfriend: "No kidding!" Satisfied to know that he is a buff dude ready to take on the challenge.

She is pleased to know that her guy is willing to defend her honor. Although they are only teenagers, most women feel this way. They want to know that their man is going to protect and fight for her honor. The male animal is oriented toward protecting life, property, and his mate. Men are called to action. Women don't really want a touchy feely man; the so-called "nice guy". Men protect the turf: the home, the wife, the children, and the business. Mom stays home and takes care of the little babes, well, that is how it used to be, and of course, still is even when she has a career. Males are turf animals. They are here to protect and defend their land, family, job, and yes, their girlfriend or wife.

The Day of the Duel

The Burr-Hamilton duel is perhaps the most famous duel in history. It was fought between two well-known politicians: Secretary of Treasury Alexander Hamilton and Vice President Aaron Burr on July 11, 1804. Both men were close in age and both had been involved in duels in the past.

The men first clashed during the election of 1800 when Aaron Burr ran against Thomas Jefferson for president and unfortunately tied Thomas Jefferson. Each man had 65 votes a piece. The election was then moved to the House of Representatives where Alexander Hamilton did his best to convince everyone that Jefferson was the better candidate even though he did not really like him. (He just liked Aaron Burr less.) Jefferson won. Burr was hardly the loser in the whole deal as he ended up being vice president which was close enough. It was a pretty impressive job to have. Any man would be happy with it.

At one point, Aaron Burr obtained and published "The Public Conduct and Character of John Adams, Esq., President of the United States," written by Alexander Hamilton which went on to harass Adams. It was meant for private eyes. Alexander Hamilton did not stop there. He once again went against Burr during the 1804 governor's race in New York where he tried to convince Federalists not to vote for Burr. That was it!

Burr would have been perfectly happy to receive an apology from Alexander Hamilton; however, none was received which forced the two men to defend his individual honor. Their "seconds" (official assistants) tried to resolve any hurt feelings before the issue got too out of hand. Neither man seemed to be interested.

As any great statesman would do, Hamilton carefully prepared his eulogy the evening before, just in case. The next morning each offended party climbed into separate boats and rowed across the Hudson River to Weehawken, New Jersey. Their 16 inch flintlock pistols were transported separately. Printed warfare had turned into the real thing. Both men stood facing each other to settle personal and political differences. One man was not particularly good at shooting, but he showed to seek justice and as expected, the shot missed its target. The other mark was hit and Alexander died the next day.

Since duels were in the process of being outlawed, Aaron Burr was charged with two counts of murder and he was never to hold office again. However, the charges were later dismissed. The duel between Hamilton and Burr forever sealed their reputations. According to folks, Hamilton was "a saint, a martyr while Burr was a murderous psychopath". Never mind that they both agreed to the challenge.

Duels had rules. It is not as if two fellows took a shot at each other. It was an educated man's way of bringing justice to a situation. Any respectable man would agree to the rules lest their insolence be published in the local paper for all to see. Besides, poppin' off a man had its benefits. It was immediate. It was certainly fair, and it took care of justice in one shot, sometimes more if the fellow missed his mark. The church, however, in no way supported pistol packing duels or justice at the tip of a sword and felt it was best to leave justice to God.

The duel was the final judge for many things: debts, honesty, land ownership, defending a fair female's honor or insult, or any offense against his horse. He could also be challenged for calling the man a liar, cheat, or worse yet, a coward. One might be able to settle with an apology as long as the affront was not too bold. The offended might demand an apology first. If the offender felt he was in the wrong, he could respectfully issue an apology. Even President Andrew Jackson's mother told him that he should never take an insult. He should fight to defend his honor. Interestingly, she was related to Robert the Bruce, the fellow that took up the Scottish hero William Wallace's cause. Must have run in the bloodline.

Instead of the sight of "red wet blood", (a bloody nose would probably be far more satisfying to the offended) insults are now settled through judgments; impersonal at best. A fist fight in a bar late at night between two sweaty drunks might be considered a modern duel, however, those who have suffered an affront will undoubtedly find themselves hauled to the slammer where they will have the night to ponder any insult. As much as modern politicians and lawmakers try to legislate human behavior, the task is nearly impossible. Humans are who they are. Men are geared to fight and protect and defend. No laws in the world will be able to tame testosterone, that powerful hormone that makes a man a man.

Gone are the days of men settling their differences by steel blade or by pistol. Gone also are the days when cafes kept a stock of swords and other such weaponry for men who meant to satisfy offenses in a timely manner. Today's grievances sit in a pile on a desk in the courthouse waiting their turn for a judge's decision. Hardly a satisfying ending. It would be much better to settle with fists, unfortunately young men who choose this method often find themselves confined to a cell awaiting the judge's decision.

Swords were once the receptacle for a man's word, his honor, his dedication, his service, his defense, or his loyalty. A knight pledged his fidelity to his king and queen upon his sword. A son pledged his honor to his father's sword. A soldier or his family placed his sword over the mantle of his fireplace as a testimony to a well-fought battle. And besides, blades left scars. Scars were confirmation that one's honor had been defended. Scars were a visible reminder that a man had honored his reputation.

A sword was a part of one's soul. Your very life depended on it. A man felt a loyalty and love towards his sword. Some men had names for their favorite blade. The old original war sword was so massive it sometimes required both hands to use. Wearing a sword like this advertized how tall you were. "Four feet of steal hanging from your waist and you swaggering around with it, made quite a statement!" According to a recent story, a hockey player's skate almost decapitated a player's head as it slid across his neck. Imagine the blade of a finally sharpened sword.

Judge Andrew Scott had great respect for the ladies. He felt it his duty to protect a woman's reputation. He attended a party where Judge Joseph Selden was also present. While playing a game of cards a lady exclaimed she had "the tricks and honors on him!" (In other words, she was winning.) Selden remarked that he didn't think so, which in turn hurt her feelings terribly. Judge Scott sprung to her defense declaring that Judge Selden should apologize and threw a candlestick in his face. Selden did send her an apology, but it was too late. Scott and Selden met to settle the situation. It ended with poor Judge Selden slumping to the ground; the lady's honor having been restored. It didn't seem to matter that she had accepted his apology.

Courage was the hallmark of a gentleman even if he was a bad boy. Alexander McClung of Kentucky was fondly dubbed the Black Night of the South. "He was a handsome dark-eyed redhead and the bad boy of a respectable family". He gave little to his profession of choice as dueling seemed to engage more than the courtroom. He had a major hand in eliminating several of the Menifee's of Kentucky. His partner was a black horse named Rob Roy and every bit as reckless as his owner. He tried studying medicine and law, but poets are free spirits and cannot be tied down to the mundane monotony of everyday life.

McClung also has the dubious distinction of being the nephew of Chief Justice John Marshall, but grew up fatherless. He was a renegade poet, if there is such a thing; a dueling demon from a well-bred family, with the temperament of the devil himself. He came into an inheritance at age twenty-one which he fluttered away before his next birthday. Maybe it was the cape he wore at times that gave him a sense of immortality. Capes seem to do that to men.

He was one of those boys that the service could not tame and he soon departed with the navy, not on his terms, however. (He was asked to leave.) McClung could make friends if he wanted to and did so with a fellow named General Allen, but after a minor falling out between the friends, Allen declared McClung to be a "liar, scoundrel, and fool" in front of everybody.

They met along the Pearl River where Allen fired and missed. McClung shouted to his one time friend, "Are you content?"

"NO!" shouted the General who reached for another pistol. McClung then informed him he would hit him right in the teeth. The General seemed to not take notice and the shot was fired. The bullet seared through Allen's teeth and lodged in his neck. After that, the Black Knight's reputation was sealed. No one dared tamper with the redheaded dare devil, yet many women swooned for the copper headed dueler although he was no gentleman regardless for his love of fine poetry. One source says that he once fought seven brothers and killed all of them, but stories do tend to get more glamorous as they are passed around or maybe it was the cape.

After a stint in the Mexican War and no one willing to meet his challenge of a duel anymore (his reputation was his own worst enemy), the bottle became his friend wrangling his spirit away from him and his drinking overtook him. He had a carpenter make a chair with a deep V slashed into the top. One day McClung positioned his neck into groove of the slot and shot himself in the head in a hotel in Jackson, Mississippi. His final words forever immortalized in a poem, of course. The last line crying, "O death, Come soon! Come soon!" He never seemed to lack drama.

During one particular duel, an ugly fellow lopped off the nose of a handsome fellow who bent over to retrieve his appendage only to have it stomped into the ground by his rival. Then there is the story of a writer who told an Officer of the Guard that he smelled like a goat. When the officer challenged him he replied, "Put up you sword, you fool." If you kill me you will not smell any better, and if I kill you, you will smell much worse."

The composer of the Star Spangled Banner, Francis Scott Key, had a son named Daniel who got into it over how fast two steamboats were traveling. The other fellow disagreed naturally and the duel was set up. Daniel was only twenty-years-old.

Then there was the famous duel between a fellow named Peter Van Allen and William H. Crawford a politician who was not only Secretary of War, but also a well-known statesman whose face appeared on the 50 cent note.

A squabble began between General John Clark and William Crawford over whether or not Clark should be entitled to some land for getting rid of some pesky Indians. Van Allen, a professional duelist and political opponent of Crawford's was brought in to verbally rough up Crawford a bit. Before he knew it, the portly politician found himself facing an opponent he had no quarrel with. The slick Van Allen stood like a taunting child making ridiculous faces at his opponent which really had nothing to do with anything. Crawford fired missing his target who deserved at this point to be the recipient of his bullet. Peter Van Allen popped off a shot as well, also missing his mark. Crawford then pulled his hat brim down so as not to be distracted by the childish antics of the professional duelist a second time. It worked. The shot rang out and Van Allen wilted to the ground. The statesman not only was vindicated, but enjoyed increased popularity.

One duel included a fellow with a wooden leg. To be fair, (after all that's was dueling was all about, dignity and honor) his opponent placed his leg in a hollow gum tree. Now the men were on (pardon the pun) equal footing. After all, a man had his principles. He certainly did not want to win unfairly.

There is the story of the Hatfields and McCoys, perhaps the most famous feud of all. The back hills hillbillies whose immortality has been portrayed or mimicked almost to the point of exhaustion in movies and television. The scuffle first began over hogs, which in turn developed into a feud that would last for 13 years. The court decided for the Hatfields. The McCoys thought the whole thing quite unfair and ambushed a group of Hatfields which prompted a Hatfield to fire at a couple of McCoys who returned fire killing the Hatfield.

Then Roseanna McCoy fell in love with of all things, a Hatfield. Johnse and Roseanna lived together for a spell before she decided to move back. Sadly, love with a Hatfield was not quite what she thought it would be. Apparently, Johnse was quite the looker and didn't want to waste all of his manly appeal on just one lady. No one likes to see their woman slam the door behind her, but Johnse didn't seem to notice. Of course, Roseanna's father, Ole Ran'l McCoy, was deeply offended by the whole thing, but mostly because Johnse was a Hatfield.

Soon the Hatfields and McCoys were picking each other off like corn on a cob. Bad blood between the clans went on regardless of the short lived romance. The National Guard and the state governors got involved. The feud ended up traveling all the way to the Supreme Court. Interestingly, William Anderson Hatfield's (aka Devil Anse) nephew Henry became governor of West Virginia and United States Senator. I guess they weren't all bad.

The Expedition of Humphry Clinker is a novel written by Tobias Smollet which was published in 1771. Mr. Humphry Clinker, the prominent character of the story, gets into duel with the Officer of the Horse Guard for "turning aside to the park wall on a necessary occasion, when he was passing with a lady under his protection". Walls were the recipients of a full bladder and even today in Paris one can still men participating in the art of "watering" the wall.

Jim Bowie was an adventurer who met his fate at the Battle of the Alamo. In 1832, he boarded a steamer called Orleans headed for Natchez. A young man who was traveling the same steamer looked to throw himself overboard. Bowie stepped in to rescue the man from his folly. Apparently the young fellow had been carrying 60,000 dollars which had been entrusted to him. Well, all it took was a poker game to pluck the money from the youthful fellow's pocket by a couple of card sharks. Despaired at the thought of having lost a fortune which was not his, he stood teetering above the dark watery grave below. Bowie assured the young man's wife not to worry, sauntered in and sat down at the table.

In those days, the game of poker was a slippery process, a game in which one did not always know if he would make it out a alive lest he was caught cheating and as the story would have it a player was indeed caught red handed.

Bowie spied the dealer sliding a card to the thief, whipped out his knife, and placed it against the scoundrel's person. Taken aback, the surprised card player did not recognize whom he had attempted to cheat. "Who are you?" demanded the man. From the darkness came the answer "Jim Bowie." They say ignorance is bliss, but in this case, ignorance was no man's friend and the third swindler, who had never heard of him, offered a challenge. Jim Bowie was a hardy rough fellow; a man who could rope an alligator. Both parties armed with pistols headed for the deck. Each man faced the other balancing on opposite wheel-houses which housed the large paddle wheels.

The fired shot echoed through the air, the bullet hit its target causing the rascal to flop into the river. The grateful young couple was once again in possession of the lost fortune.

In the legendary Sandbar Fight, Bowie found himself serving as a second for his friend Samuel Wells who had a disagreement with a Dr. Thomas Maddox. Both fellows missed their mark and decided to call it even with a handshake, the only gentlemanly thing to do. The spectators were not pleased, however, with the outcome and began brawling amongst themselves. Bowie found himself amidst the scuffle and was shot and eventually impaled. Furious, Bowie grabbed his knife while his attacker was trying to pull a sword from his chest, reached up, and sliced the bowels of the enemy with his blade. Another assailant found himself cut up like a pork roast at a Sunday dinner.

Involved in several other confrontations with his knife, Bowie's ability to ward off attackers became legendary and sealed his reputation by immortalizing the "bowie knife". Today the blade of a bowie knife has a measurement of 8.25 inches, a few inches short of its original size.

As folks began to move west, status became a little less important having been replaced by tough fisted real men not fancy dandies from cotton plantations. In Missouri, the duelist was the "favorite of the fair." Mr. Charles Lucas was an aristocrat from Pennsylvania. Thomas Benton from Missouri grew up fatherless. Benton thought Charles Lucas was an effeminate snob. Lucas thought Thomas Benton was a barbarian. Mr. Lucas suffered from the "immortal twenties" as most young men do when youth over powers common sense. Neither fellow had much use for the other. As it happened, both men's careers were on the rise and one day they found themselves on opposite sides in court. Each thought the other a liar and butted heads over a point of evidence.

At one point, Lucas accused Benton of not being able to legally vote. The attorney claimed he did indeed own property, paid taxes, and was able to vote. Mr. Benton went on further claiming that Lucas was making ridiculous charges and told him, 'I will not answer any charges made by any puppy who happens to run across my path.' Well, as you know, that's all it took. "Puppy was a fighting word".

Charles Lucas sent his second, Joshua Barton, to invite Mr. Benton to meet with him. Said Benton, "I never quarrel, sir, but I do fight, sir, and when I fight, sir, a funeral follows, sir." They met on Bloody Island to settle the matter. It was only semantics, but being called a puppy was not a good thing. Mr. Benton took a wound to his knee and Mr. Lucas suffered a bullet to the throat narrowly missing the jugular vein.

Six weeks later, as a matter of etiquette, the two met again. (Benton had been accused of cheating the first time.) Much like the knight's code, duels had rules, a code of etiquette if you will. Half the town of St Louis gasped in disbelief as the honorable Thomas Benton rolled up his sleeves to expose red flannel underwear. Whether it was to throw Lucas off or he was really cold, the day was steamy and stifling, for whatever reason, there stood Benton in all his glory waiting for the count. Both fired at once. As Lucas collapsed, in his last breath he whispered, 'I forgive you, Sir.' While Lucas met his fate at the tender age of 25, Benton went on to become one of Missouri's first senators and lived to the respectable age of 76.

There is the story of Mark Twain and his brush with a duel although he preferred to settle matters by pen. He was not one much for duels and even once commented on the Alexander Hamilton duel. Alexander, whom Twain declared to be "high-principled", fought the duel anyway because of public opinion.

Twain's editorial reviews could at times be droll and even a bit sarcastic and not everyone admired his cleverness with the pen. One reader was so incensed by a particular editorial that he threatened to kick Twain all the way across Nevada. Twain's reply, "Well, if you think you have enough money to put me all over these toll roads, just start in!" Twain had a way of doing that, offending even the most unoffended. After a nasty falling out with a publisher by the name of James Laird, the man who considered duels "unwise and dangerous" challenged Laird to a duel.

Marksmanship was not the same as penmanship and Twain couldn't hit the door on the side of a barn even it was red. After a few practice shots it was clear that Twain had gotten himself into a mess. Steven Gillis, his second, popped off the head of a bird congratulating Twain on such a good hit as Laird and his friends arrived. The men's eyes scanned the little bird's head wondering who could have done such a thing. Gillis informed the men that Twain had done it. Needless to say, thanks to the author's quick thinking second, Twain avoided a brush with death that day. One duel was enough for Twain; however, he retained his interest in other's squabbles as dueling was still seen as a necessary thing to do.

Duels are seen as heroic events, yet a sinful, stupid thing by others. One can certainly see the appeal of a duel; it was dangerous, yet daring, sinful yet solemn, dramatic and many times illegal, which of course, only enhanced its appeal even further. After all, it is human nature to want to be a bit naughty even if it meant having a hole blown through your person. Your grave marker no doubt hailed you as a hero, a man's man; a fellow who met the call to a challenge and died bravely. The graveyards were full of men who were no coward, but dead heroes nonetheless.

According to author Barbara Holland, "If Abraham Lincoln and Jefferson Davis had faced each other with pistols a half of million lives could have been saved minus one and a whole lot of money". Maybe dueling wasn't such a bad thing.

In England, duels were illegal, but no one was really punished for engaging in a dispute. Meeting the challenge became more of something one had to do: you showed up, you fired your pistol, you shook hands, you went home. And if the challenger had any rank or importance at all he got his name in the paper. Duels became protocol rather than an actual confrontation where one pointed a pistol at another hoping to get his point across.

"Different spanks for different ranks" seemed to be the code among French and English soldiers. Officers could fight, but enlisted men were punished for doing so. A dispute arose between two officers, one claiming the beer to be much better in his regiment and one accusing the other man of being a scoundrel. Lt. Evans demanded an apology from Lt. Ogilvy and received none. As with most duels, there was a clear winner, the dead man being Lt. Ogilvy who could not make himself apologize over whose beer was better.

Then there was the case of a Mr. Nesbit who was accused of really being a woman by a Mr. Broadstreet. Nesbit challenged the accuser as any red blooded male would do since being called a girl in any form is an insult to a male's sensibility. By order of the governor, Mr. Nesbit was ordered to receive a thorough examination. The thought of having his person invaded caused Mr. Nesbit to break down. But, alas! It was indeed true. Mr. Nesbit was really a "Miss Nevile" who then had no choice but to leave the service. Thank goodness, no blood was spilled.

By now, the duel had been floundering for some time. There were those who thought them foolish, those who thought justice should be left to the courts, and those who had witnessed the tangled mess of lives and limbs during the civil war and felt enough honor had been sacrificed. At one time boys as young as fourteen stood facing a challenge to their father's pride and approval. Possible death was nothing compared to a fellow's honor and good name. Legal penalties for dueling did not exist, however. Public humiliation and your name printed in the local paper for being a coward was enough for a man to accept a challenge. There was nothing "Beyond that of his heart, his sword, and his valor". But duels went the way of the code of the knight and disappeared into the pages of history replaced by the antics of the legendary outlaws of the Wild West: Wyatt Earp, the Younger Brothers, Jesse James, and Billy the Kid.

Lying today has many definitions: hype, spin, cover-up, libel, "public relations", or waffling. One dares not lie under oath, but lying is everywhere. Trying to control falsehoods today with the mass use of the internet is like trying to shove a tornado back into a cloud. They keep swirling around until they become so powerful and so out of control that it is impossible to distinguish between the truth and a story. Mendacious men are nearly impossible to control. Unfortunately, once a vicious lie has been put out for all to see, trying to recover one's good reputation usually entails hiring one of those no-nonsense-take-no-prisoner lawyers to put it back in good standing. Can you imagine such a thing in a world today, face to face, man to man, your sword and skill against his or lack of, fighting for honor and one's reputation and dignity?

Today anyone seems to be able to say anything on the internet or airwaves whether it is true or not and it immediately travels the world in a split second. The old rules of edict would be nearly impossible to enforce in a technical computer world. Bring back the sword! Dueling with hand held weapons to settle an affront has been replaced by the modern legal system and romanticized in modern movies and stories. But men do still have the right to bear arms. An armed man feels better about himself; taller and braver, not necessarily above public law, but ready to supplement it with a private one.

The Right to Bear Arms is specifically stated in the Constitution of the United States of America. The second amendment in the United States Constitution grants citizens the right to keep and bear arms. The Second amendment of the United States Constitution further states: A well regulated Militia, being necessary to the security of a free state, grants the right to its citizens the right to keep and bear arms shall not be infringed.

The right to keep and bear arms came from the mother country herself before folks left England to settle the colonies. Citizens in the thirteen original colonies were allowed to maintain personal firearms as it was a part of the common law heritage. Oh, the British tried to prevent folks from owning guns (a common theme trying to be employed today), but the colonists would have none of it.

One of the hardest decisions for the men who wrote the Constitution was allowing the Federal government to maintain a standing army. While important to national security, it could also be a problem to one's freedom. The decision was made to have an army that was under civilian control. The American Revolution was won because citizens were armed with guns so it would have hardly been of any benefit to a brand new country to take away their guns. Guns serve to protect citizens from both foreign, governmental, and domestic invasion. Men in good physical health and standing should know how to use a gun as well as owning one.

According to Sir William Blackstone, who was an "authoritative voice" of common law in the colonies, "citizens were therefore entitled to exercise their natural right of resistance and self-preservation, when the sanctions of society and laws are found insufficient to restrain the violence of oppression." Blackstone not only believed in the individual's right to have and use arms, but further believed that for its defense a nation should rely not on a standing army, but the citizen soldier. Plainly, for such a concept to be a reality, it is necessary that all able-bodied males possess and be capable of using arms.

When the United States was a young country, its citizens were the protectors and defenders. Anyone who has studied this country's history knows the sacrifice its citizens underwent to protect their freedom. Today, we the citizens of this great country have the right to bear arms whether those who want to deny men of their guns like it or not.

According to a statistic, 1 in 3 employees want to leave their jobs because of an annoying co-worker. Maybe the workplace should keep a stash of swords in the closet.

CHAPTER 6
GREAT WARRIORS

At the age of seven Spartan boys were trained in the art of war. The young trainees were made to sleep naked in the middle of the winter and walk barefoot on long marches. The boys were beaten on a regular basis to see how much pain they could endure. Young boys were pitted against each other one on one unarmed and would go days practicing drills often with little rest or food and sometimes no water. It was a test of individual wills and strength. The youthful group would form a line with each youth pressing his shield into the boy in front of him. Such force was then applied to a tree. The pressure of the line against the tree was so great that it pushed the tree over. Many times someone was killed during this "exercise".

"Revolution, reform, and rebellion" appeal to men. Nothing can match the camaraderie of men who have stood shoulder to shoulder in the heat of battle. Your life is at the mercy of the man who stands beside you. This is an aspect of war that many people do not understand. Nobody likes to kill another human being, but there is more to war. A scholar of history, Sir William Tarn states that Alexander the Great invaded Persia because "he never thought of not doing it".

The Macedonian army was a professional army composed of highly trained men. These men were proud to be Macedonians and their skills reflected their pride. What made the army so formidable was that the military men were professionals who trained all year round as soldiers. Macedonians possessed good will and high moral among the men. Few things are more satisfying than having a purpose, sharing it with others, and accomplishing the goal. These were tough, prepared, athletic men. The mere sight of the marching Macedonians was enough to send villagers scattering in terror. The Persians were as proud and brave as the Macedonians. Their traditional weapon was the bow and their leaders took great delight in personal combat.

The success of the military can be attributed to solid leadership. Alexander's men watched every move he made. Alexander knew the importance of his role. While inspecting his troops he would remove his helmet to show his vulnerability, a sight that endeared him to his men. "I am one of you," the gesture said. He was a genius military leader who never lost a battle. In 12 years he conquered most of the known territories to the Greeks.

While Alexander the Great has been glamorized throughout history and in modern movies, he was not above inflicting great brutality upon his enemy. He treated women well, but his enemies with extreme cruelty. One by the name of Batris, although gravely injured, was tied to a chariot and drug around a wall.

The Battle of Gaugamela took place in 331 B.C. and was one of the most spectacular battles Alexander fought. The Macedonians met the forces of Darius III of Persia. Darius was attempting to stop Alexander's troops who were sorely outnumbered. He was in possession of 40,000 infantry and 7,000 cavalry as opposed to Darius who was in possession of 200,000 infantry, 40,000 Calvary, and 6,000 Greek mercenaries. Alexander was able to outmaneuver Darius which in turn left a gap in the center of the battle line exposed. Alexander and his personal cavalry immediately rushed in. Darius and some of his troops managed to escape, but he was eventually caught and murdered. Shortly after, Gaugamela, Alexander was crowned "King of Asia".

Among the many wounds that Alexander the Great sustained during battle was a cleaver slash to head, arrow through his leg, arrow lodged in his lung, and a catapult missile to the chest. He eventually contracted a fever whether by poison or the fact that he had suffered so many injuries is not known. He was a heavy drinker which probably contributed to his eventual demise.

Aristotle was Alexander the Great's Teacher.

Geronimo

Just hearing the words "Apache Indian" conjures up the image of a ferocious band of warriors cutting down everything in their path.

The Apaches were the last group of Native Americans to put up a fight against the expanding white man. Upon the end of the Civil War, the government now turned its attention to the Native Americans. Many were captured and placed on reservations, which were gradually decreased in size; a policy that infuriated the Apaches.

Geronimo was born in New Mexico in 1829 and by 1858 had become one of the fiercest of all warriors. He originally lived in the region which is now New Mexico. Geronimo was a Bedonkohe Apache who married into the Chiricahuas. When his wife and children were murdered Geronimo swore he would extinguish the white man and for the next several decades this became his goal. Although only a medicine man, his ferocity in which he fought the white man percolates all kinds of images in the modern mind: fierce warrior, avenger for the death of his family, leader of the Apaches.

He rounded up a collection of renegades and raided New Mexico, Arizona, and northern Mexico. His exploits became highly chronicled by the press and he became the most feared Apache. Geronimo and his band were eventually captured at Skeleton Canyon in 1886. The Chiricahua Apache were then shipped by rail to Ft. Madison in St. Augustine, Florida.

Seeing a way to exploit their captive, some businessmen had Geronimo shipped to Fort Pickens in Pensacola, Florida in October of 1886. The idea was to keep him under a more watchful eye in case he should pull anything devious. The great warrior ended up a spectacle put on display as he slaved away at hard labor while curiosity seekers gawked. Eventually he headed to the St. Louis World's fair where he signed autographs and had his picture taken with tourists. He died in 1909. A warrior does not belong as a curiosity in a side show.

The mark of manhood, the very essence of what a man is proved through his triumphs: defeating enemies, winning wars, and staking victory in sports competitions. The battlefield has been a place where men have displayed their courage, leadership abilities, strength, dominance, athletic prowess, and honor. Those same attributes can be seen in the workplace, at the gym, or on the athletic field.

Medieval and renaissance England is a period in history when men were men. They fought, they protected, and defended. They ruled. They adhered to a code of honor and worked hard to maintain their manliness. They fought battles without star wars equipment; hand to hand and face to face combat. They engaged in tremendous athletic feats like jousting; a sport where two opponents would race head on towards each other to win a lady's approval.

Men have lived and died by a code of honor. Slavery was stopped by the strength of men. The Nazis were stopped by men of courage.

Just before he went down in 1940, a British pilot and member of the Royal Air Force wrote, "The universe is so vast and so ageless that the life of one man can only be justified by the measure of his sacrifice".

What makes great historical figures of days gone by such as William Wallace so endearing to the 21st century man is that he fought for a cause. Braveheart moves people because the man knew why he was here. He did not relent; he fought, and died for a purpose. He did not read the papers to see what the latest poll said. He did not cower beneath a politically correct agenda. He did not ask permission from a political body whether it would be okay if he roughed up the English a bit. He did not check with feminists of the time to see if it was not nice to go after Edward Longshanks or be labeled a "bully". What he did do was fight for Scotland's freedom. What he had was a purpose.

Men were created to lead. At one time, soldiers who returned from war were applauded in the airports, rewarded with medals, and in the case of battles gone by, given parades to honor the brave men who defended our liberties, preserved our Constitution, and country. Men are willing to give up life and limb for their country. The military provides something that is sadly lacking in today's world. A sense of honor and duty. Wars are fought by men of every nationality, religion, and color. The Civil War was fought by all colors including 200,000 men who were African Americans.

Sir Winston Churchill, "If we can stand up to him, Hitler, all Europe maybe free and the life of the world may move forward into broad, sunlit uplands. But if we fail, then the whole world, including the United States, including all that we have known and care for, will sink into the abyss of a new Dark Age more sinister, and perhaps more protected by the light of perverted science. Let is therefore brace ourselves to our duties, and so bear ourselves that, if the British Empire and Commonwealth last for a thousand years, men will say, "This was their finest hour." Bravery comes in many forms.

Imagine the politically correct crowd harassing the President over the dropping of the bomb over Hiroshima. Imagine WWII soldiers trying to defend the United States and having the media looking over their shoulder ready to record their actions to vilify the man on national TV instantaneously. War is not a clean event, nor is it a fair event, nor an event that can always be politically correct.

Sir Ernest Henry Shackleton was born February 15, 1874 in Ireland and died in 1922. He is best remembered today for his Antarctic expedition of 1914. It was called the "Discovery Expedition", after his ship called *The Discovery*. Associated with this expedition is the myth that Shackleton posted this message in December of 1901:

"Men wanted for hazardous journey. Small wages. Bitter cold. Long months of winter. Constant danger. Safe return doubtful. Honour and recognition in case of success". 5000 men showed up.

This makes a great story and an intriguing tale of adventures gone by. Men are pack animals. At one time they hunted, conquered lands, overthrew governments, provided for the village, protected their women and children, and sailed to new continents together. And in this case, trekked to the Antarctic together.

Weapons technology is important in any war and throughout time, it has either meant defeat or victory. The Romans first used chainmail armor, gunpowder was utilized in China in 1350, and firearms first used in France in 1718. Machine guns were first used in England in 1866, dynamite first in Sweden, and the airplane used first by the U.S. in 1916. The U.K. first used the tank and in 1933, radar.

Biological warfare dates back to B.C. In the 5th century B. C., Scythian archers dipped their arrows in animal dung before shooting at their targets. The dipped arrow caused the wounds to become infected. Other militias have used infected or dead soldiers which they flung over the walls of forts to infect the enemy.

Animals have been used at various times during war as well. Elephants were first used by the Carthaginians against Rome in 262 B.C., but the Romans just opened their defense line and watched the elephants run through. Other animals that have been used in wartime: rats, sea lions (used by the U.S. navy during the Iraqi War of 2003 to look for enemy frogmen) as well as ticks, pigeons, monkeys, and parrots. Oxen were once dressed in silk costumes with burning straw tied to their tales so that they resembled dragons. Scared the you-know-what out of the enemy at the siege of Jimo in 279 B.C.

Animals could also offer a tasty solution to a hungry soldier. Things that were eaten by a news correspondent during the Siege of Apris by the Germans in 1870 were roasted cats (tastes like squirrel), kitten in onion ragou, donkey steaks (resembled mutton in taste), rat salami, and spaniel slices.

It wasn't just enough to defeat the enemy. A soldier had to teach his nemesis a lesson as well, one the unlucky adversary would never forget. After the Battle of Leigniz in 1241, the Mongols collected nine sacks of ears from the defeated source and in 1300 B.C., King Menephta's army returned to Egypt with 13,000 phalluses taken from their defeated enemy, the Libyans. Ow.

A famous picture of Richard Nixon shows the former president holding up both arms spouting the victory sign. This gesture originates from English archers as they taunted the French at Agincourt in 1415. Led by Henry V at the Battle of Agincourt, 900 English men-at-arms and 5,000 archers defeated 20,000 French troops. Of course, it didn't hurt that the enemy couldn't draw a bow. The English would hold up their fingers in a "V" sign because the archers had lopped off the captured yeoman's middle and index finger which, of course, ended the enemies' career with the bow.

Many actors play heroes in movies, but some have participated in real war like actor Charles Bronson who flew 21 combat missions as a nose gunner in bombers. He served in the Pacific theater. Assigned to the 61st Bomb Squadron of the 39th Bomb Group of the Twentieth Air Force, he flew bombing missions to Japan from North Field, Guam. Jack Palance underwent facial reconstruction from injuries he suffered in 1943 when his B-17 crashed.

While Jimmy Stewart's character George in *"It's a Wonderful Life"* stays back to take care of the family business, his brother Harry goes off to be a Navy pilot and comes back a hero. In real life, Jimmy Stewart achieved the rank of Brigadier General.

While the Little General is no movie star (dead people can't be in movies), the most often portrayed person in history in the movies is the Little General himself, Napoleon.

Sylvester Stallone, the macho champion and avenger of evil villains and corrupt soldiers has perfected the movie hero who rushes in to save his men and right all that is wrong in this evil world. It works well on the screen, but in reality he worked as an athletic girls coach in France during the Vietnam War. Oh, well. On the other hand, Galusha Pennypacker was promoted to brigadier general in the U.S. army just a month before his 21st birthday in 1865.

Class ranking does not always dictate who will be a fine military leader. It is interesting to note that Robert E. Lee graduated 2nd out of 46 at West Point, Ulysses S. Grant graduated 21st out of 39, George S. Patton, 46th out of 103, Douglas MacArthur 1st out of 93 and Wesley Clark (yup, the same guy that ran for president) 1st out of 579.

Did you know that during WWI Hollywood constructed an entire American suburb with cars, houses, and painted roads out of canvas and draped it over a giant aircraft factory to fool Japanese spotter planes. It worked. Henry VIII had done a similar thing to prepare for his meeting with Francis I.

During the Middle Ages the Vikings were thought to have eaten hallucinogenic mushrooms to jump start their battle rage. While British troops were often given an extra ration of rum before an advance during WWI. During WWII, each Italian trooper in North Africa carried his own personal espresso maker. The term "jarhead" comes from World War II because the marines wore a high-collared dress uniform.

Code names given to U. S. military actions:

SEA LION Nazi invasion of Britain scheduled for 1940

ZAPATA The landing for Cuba's Bay of Pigs 1961

EAGLE CLAW United States for when they tried to rescue American hostages from the embassy in Tehran in 1980

BARBAROSSA Hitler's invasion of Russia

MARKET GARDEN Allied Airborne and ground attacks through Holland September 1944

DESERT STORM U.S. and Allied actions to expel Iraqi forces from Kuwait

The King of Spades: Winston Churchill

King of Hearts: Joseph Stalin

King of Diamonds: Franklin D. Roosevelt

King of Clubs: Charles de Gaulle

Joker: Adolph Hitler

Many people see war as the ultimate in human ugliness, yet paintings portray war as something almost beautiful. The color of exploding bombs in the sky, the mass array of colors in vivid oranges and smoky grays, and the men in their sometimes matching, sometimes ragged uniforms. There is something fascinating, almost mesmerizing, about war which can be "both exotic and strange". Faraway lands, unusual people, and scenery all add to the allure of battle.

According to J. Glenn Gray, there are three attractions to war: the delight in seeing what comes from the spectacle of battlefield encounters, the delight in comradeship and mutual willingness to engage in self-sacrifice, and the delight in destructtion.

Men are warriors. Men are proud of their scars. They are badges of honor to men. Men are naturally warriors, but in peacetime, a man who longs for an adrenal rush risks bungee jumps, drives race cars, and jumps out of airplanes. That's what boys are all about; who's bigger, who's stronger, and who's tougher and if that doesn't work, whose dad is bigger, whose dad is stronger, and whose dad is tougher.

It's a long standing truth that there is never a more devoted group of men than those who have fought alongside each other. Maybe that is what the average person does not understand about war. It's not about killing for the pleasure of it, it's about country, camaraderie, protection, honor, and deep trust; "a band of brothers". Men who share your same values and goals. Men who love their country and their fellowman. If not for millions of soldiers who have fought for our country we might speak German, French, or Spanish today. We may be living in a world ruled by the ancestors of Stalin and Hitler. We would live in a country where slavery is still legal. Many soldiers who fought for the slaves' freedom were white men. It is mostly men who stand guard at the border, men who fly fighter missions, and men who have stood eye to eye with the enemy.

The Kohima epitaph was written by John Maxwell Edwards (1875-1958). It can be seen on the WWII Memorial for the fallen Allied. This famous epitaph is found on numerous Veteran Memorials and Monuments throughout the world because a soldier knows no race, religion, or color.

When you go home, tell them of us and say,
For their tomorrow, we gave our today.

CHAPTER 7
JOHNNY DEPP IS NO PIRATE

C aptain Jack Sparrow is appealing to so many women because he "looks" like your typical pirate: adventurous, athletic, masculine looking, and a little bit naughty. A lady gets the feeling that if she smiles just right, he might take her up on it. Unfortunately, real pirates were not quite so good looking or funny. They were often morbidly cruel people who inflicted painful punishments on their captured enemy.

Piracy can be traced back thousands of years. The success of the pirate crew depended largely on their vessel and the skill with which it was employed. The ideal pirate ship of any age was quick, well armed, and capable of holding a substantial cargo of booty. It should be of no surprise that a pirate usually acquired his ship by stealing it. Speed was important as they needed to be able to out run prey and pursuers. Rarely did pirates have the means to purchase their own vessel. They typically adapted captured merchantmen or warships by cutting gun ports into the hull for extra cannons. There also had to be enough space to accommodate a large crew. They hung close to the coastline because it gave them the advantage when dealing with adversaries.

The pirate flag, also called the "Jolly Roger", comes from the French words *joli rouge* which means pretty red. Just the appearance of the pirate's symbol flapping in the gales as the ship made its way over the horizon was enough to strike the fear of God into the hearts of those who were unfortunate enough to be on the sea the same time as the approaching ruffians. Many symbols comprised the pirate's banner. The black and white skull and crossbones flag first showed upon the sea when it was raised by a French pirate. Bartholomew Robert's flag showed him and a skeleton drinking a toast to death. Black seemed to be the color of choice.

As the pirate crew made their way onto another's ship they would "vaporize" which further intimidated the unfortunate crew. The pirates would dance like clacking skeletons, a bunch of drunks swinging their cutlass' wildly as they dangled about.

Every land and country bred pirates. There were Chinese, Spanish, English, and even America pirates, but the one thing they had in common was that pirates were not nice people. These guys were dangerous and were afraid of nothing. They sailed to unknown territories for months, sometimes years, not knowing what they would find.

A pirate's life was short, but exciting and he usually ended up as a hanging decoration over a harbor; his flesh dropping off as his corpse rotted against the sea and sun.

Why would a man be attracted to such a harsh life style? Knowing he only had a few good years at the most? The possibility of discovering riches and sharing in the bounty. Interestingly, a man of the royal navy was subjected to worst discipline than a pirate whose raiding of the seas could produce tremendous personal wealth. Besides, the pirate knew his life was relatively short and to him the freedom of the seas combined with the riches that were for the taking was worth the hanging if he was caught.

While being a member of the Royal Navy sounds glamorous and impressive, many men were thrown into military service by press gangs whose job it was to find people to serve. Once aboard, the unfortunate fellow stayed aboard so that he had no chance of escape. Pirates didn't have time for the rules of the Royal Navy or any rules for the matter.

The personal weapon of choice was one that was small enough to use effectively. Pirate ships were tight spaces with little elbow room. Their favorite weapon was the cutlass which had a short thick curved blade. Most any rogue could wield a cutlass with little training. It was an excellent weapon for man to man, hand to hand confrontation or to slice through ropes and canvas. Musket and pistols were a bit cumbersome because they were tedious to load. They were far more useful as a club once the bullet had been fired. Blackbeard carried six flintlock pistols (partly for show, partly for protection) which doubled as daggers or axes. Pirate ships had only so much room. A buccaneer could hardly swing a 4 foot blade against his enemy therefore, it was just a matter of convenience to possess weapons which could be used in tight quarters.

Pirates liked their cannons. Some ships were stocked with as many as forty canons. Often the one-eyed bandits would fire "a shot" at an unsuspecting sea-faring target just to let them know they meant business, besides, the pirates didn't want to do any more damage to their own vessel than was necessary.

Pirate ships consisted of the quartermaster who supervised and steered the ship. He was first lieutenant and the Captain's right hand man who enforced his master's orders. He was like the ship's banker and took charge of dividing the booty.

The ship's navigator was known as the "artist", a man who many thought had special mysterious gifts even though the majority of navigators were poor at best.

The bosun or boatswain was responsible for the maintenance of the ship and was usually the most experienced seaman on board. The skilled cooper kept watch over containers that stored water and food so it didn't spoil or become contaminated. The sail maker sewed up wounds or corpses into a canvas for burial at sea. The job of pirate gunners or "powder monkeys" as they were called started at the age of 11.

Ships had carpenters who would use anything to fix a leak. He was expected to remake sections of the hull when the ship blew into an uninhabited beach. His professional opinion came into play when the debate was whether the crew should cast off the newly captured or keep the old prisoners. His skill came into play when a man was severely injured. He would cauterize the cut off leg or arm with a sizzling hot axe.

Musicians were considered important because they kept rhythm while the pirates performed their jobs as well as serving as entertainment during leisure time. They received one and a quarter of the booty.

Pirates had rules that they took solemnly to heart:

Every man shall have an equal vote in affairs of the moment as well as equal title to strong liquors.

The lights and candles shall be put out at eight at night

Each man shall keep his piece, cutlass, and pistols at all times clean and ready for action.

No boy or woman be amongst them, if any man is found carrying his lady to sea in disguise he shall suffer death.

He that shall desert the ship in time of battle shall suffer death by marooning.

No one shall strike another on board of the ship; every man's quarrel shall end on shore by pistol or sword.

The captain and quartermaster receive two shares of the prize. Master gunner and bosun receive one and one half shares Other officers, one and one quarter. Private gentlemen of fortune, one share of the prize.

Pirate Captains did not find disobedience from the crew of any sort acceptable. Legend has it that pirates forced their victims to walk the plank although this was rare. Pirates of the 17th and 18th century would feed their captives to the sharks, however. Punishment for murder by one crewmember against another would be to tie the victim to the murderer and hurl them both overboard. Marooning a fellow pirate left him on a deserted island sometimes naked with no provisions. Almost no one who was subjected to being abandoned survived.

Pirates who committed minor offenses were given a lashing by each crewmember. A cat-o'-nine tails was a vicious whipping apparatus consisting of nine strands of knotted rope. Any crewman who dared to incur the wrath of his captain was whipped with the device. The poor victim had to make his own punishing device which he was flogged with. The tool was to be used only once because the blood splattered rope was ripe with infection.

Keelhauling consisted of dragging a wrongdoer on a rope from one side of a vessel to the other under the keel as a form of punishment. The unfortunate subject of this penalty was hoisted up on the end of the main yard where he was dangled by the wrists and a weight tied to his feet. He was run under the hull and up to the other end of the main yard then run under the hull and barnacle-covered keel. Such measures insured the pealing and scraping of the skin on the back of the victim until he was bloody. A rag soaked in oil was tied over his nose and mouth to prevent him from drowning and to ensure he felt the full effects of his punishment.

Some pirates were "gentlemen". Queen Elizabeth I's favorite "sea dog" was Sir Francis Drake. The later part of Elizabeth I's reign saw new adventures and discoveries of new lands. The Queen was first introduced to Sir Francis Drake through Sir Francis Walsingham, who along with the Earl of Leicester, and Sir Christopher Hatton, had invested in the privateer's adventures. Drake was a rough fellow who liked to do things his own way. (Which meant confiscating things that were not his.) The English were very proud of him. One of his trips included sailing through the straights of Magellan, up the coast of South America. In September 1580, after sailing around the world, Sir Francis Drake sailed back to England with a ship full of Spanish treasure. A fellow seaman, John Hawkins, had also returned from a trip to Africa loaded with gold, silver, and pearls.

Gentleman or no gentleman, the Spanish were not impressed and considered Drake the "master thief of the unknown world". While the English were delighted with their new found hero, the Spanish were particularly hostile towards Drake whom they referred to as "El Draque" or "The Dragon". Philip of Spain saw Drake as nothing more than a pirate. (Which he was.) But Elizabeth also hated the Spanish and saw nothing wrong with helping herself to their valuables.

Drake was fondly referred to by the Queen as "her pirate". She knighted him in 1581. Fortunately, for Spain, Drake died in 1596 and was buried at sea. Aside from harassing the Spanish, Drake was the first Englishmen to sail around the world; a feat which endeared him to the English who considered him a national hero.

Other pirates were scoundrels of the seas. The notorious Edward Teach was nicknamed "Blackbeard". Edward Teach was born in Bristol. His career as a privateer soon turned into one of a pirate by the early 1700's. He was a towering giant compared to most men of the day standing 6'4". Dressed in a red jacket, he wore a string of pistols around his waist. He was a pirate whose mere presence with his Charles Manson eyes and flaming beard (which he lit himself for dramatic effect) scared the life out of anyone who dared to cross him.

His braided beard hung in "pigtails" to his chest each one tied with a colorful ribbon. Under his hat he hid a hemp cord which he lit during battle. He was a bit of a dandy who enjoyed wearing colorful clothes and silk sashes. His presence scared the bejeebers even out of his own men who thought he was the devil himself. His favorite drink was rum laced with gunpowder. Blackbeard's philosophy was a drunk ship is a happy ship. Legend has it Blackbeard had as many as fourteen wives, the youngest being sixteen years old.

The notorious pirate was not particularly mean and upon retrieving desired valuables from a captured ship would allow the crew to sail on unless they caused any problems at which he would kill them or maroon them. Blackbeard had no use for Stede Bonnet and relished poking fun at pirate Stede Bonnet's poor seamanship. Once when they met off the Carolinas, Bonnet came on board and got hopelessly drunk. Blackbeard played a trick on him by getting his crew to vote another man captain of Stede's ship the *Revenge*. Shortly after, the werewolf of the seas abandoned several crew members marooning them on a deserted ledge whereupon Bonnet quickly rescued the men from certain starvation.

The barmy pirate was eventually caught up with November 22, 1718 by two royal navy sloops. During a bloody battle, he took several bullets and sustained numerous sword slashes. He was then promptly beheaded and his head hung from the ship's bowsprit, the beam that rises out from the bow of the ship, where it dangled like a Chinese lantern.

Major Stede Bonnet was born in Barbados in 1689. Born of English plantation owners, a life of piracy must have held more to the imagination with its promises of riches. He was a pretty boy who served more as a decoration to his ship than a competent captain. He was like the child who wanted to run away with the circus, but instead he chose the life of a pirate. Rare among the robbers at sea, Bonnet actually purchased his ship which he named the *Revenge* and set sail unto new adventures. At one point he met up with Blackbeard where they worked together plundering the seas until he was regulated to "guest" aboard his own ship by Blackbeard.

Eventually "the gentleman pirate" was pardoned and served as a privateer against the Spanish, but the lure of gold and treasure beckoned him back to piracy. Stede Bonnet was eventually captured and hung.

America's own version of the pirate was the privateer who rendered assistance to the Continental Navy when needed. In America, a "pirate" was a "privateer". Captain (William) Kidd was a privateer whose duty was to protect Anglo American trade routes in the Caribbean against France and is rumored to have buried his treasure on Long Island outside of New York. Murder charges were eventually brought up against Kidd and he was convicted and hanged. His corpse was thrown into an iron cage and hung over the Thames in London as a reminder to would-be pirates their fate if caught. Privateers often fought for the defense of their country, but it didn't hurt if the captured ships came loaded with booty which made the men very rich.

For the few who lived and survived the life of a pirate and grew tired of it, the issue thus became how to get out of the life with your head still intact. The Captain might be kind enough to write a get–out-of-being a pirate "ticket" which stated the poor fellow was forced into the life of a pirate. Didn't work. The British harbors were festooned with hanging rotted corpses as a warning. A pirate's life was indeed "a merry life, but a short one".

"Why join the navy if you can be a pirate?" – Steve Jobs

Section III

The Augusta National Golf Club And Other Thoughts On Sports

CHAPTER 8
GO KART RACING IS NOT A SPORT

There were several couples waiting to claim their car at a go-kart track. After watching the cars go round and round the race cars finally came to a stop. Each lady climbed into her car, after picking her favorite color of course, and commenced to putting around the tire studded raceway waving merrily to their men as they scooted around the miniature track.

Meanwhile, the guys were surveying the length of the track, how many times they were going to get to go around, which car was the fastest, and which car was the slowest. As the women climbed out, the men raced for their chosen car and hopped in. At the signal, the drivers tore out running neck in neck with the exception of one poor guy whose car (remember he chose it) crawled around the track while his buddies ran circles around him. The ladies were howling with laughter as their heroes scurried around the track nosing in and out of empty spaces. Finally one of the guys dropped back to give his friend a push while the other two raced side by side to the finish line. Winning was important. Bragging rights were necessary. The best driver needed to be acknowledged, of course. Skills were commented upon and helpful suggestions offered for the next race. And yes, there was a winner.

The male is geared for competition. There was nothing unordinary about their behavior. They were only behaving as men are supposed to behave: who's the biggest, who's the strongest, and in this case, who's the fastest. Anything can be made a competition out of even if it is driving a little toy car. The world of sports is appealing to so many men because sports are competitive, build character, muscle, strength, persistence, and camaraderie.

Did you know that only 6 to 7% of high school football players go on to play in college? About 8% of those eligible college football and basketball players are drafted by the pros and only 2 % of those guys sign a professional contract? The average career span for professional athletes is 7 years for a major league baseball player, 4 years for the national football leaguer and 3 to 4 years for a player in the National Basketball Association.

The average life expectancy of a former football player is 56 years although most males can expect to live to about the age of 70. Hard hitting has its price. While it may appear to the average recumbent recliner athlete those behemoths guarding the field may look like they enjoy bashing the entrails out of their opponents, most do not relish the idea of being battered about nor do they get pleasure from having the oxygen knocked out of them. Aggression goes hand in hand with the game. There is hurting to hurt and there is being tough and aggressive to play the game well and win as long as it is in a controlled environment with rules. Not anger induced. Competitive sports, especially professional sports, can come with a hefty price tag on a man's health and body.

Men love the camaraderie associated with sports teams. They love the fact that sports are open to everyone. Anyone with ability and a willingness to work hard can achieve great things. Sports are patriotic. Football is a very American game. Sports are aggressive. A fan can watch and live vicariously through his favorite player or team while not having to take the hits. Many people have found athletics to be fun, a place to build friendships or push their bodies toward excellence, where they get a sense of identification and a shared goal. Valuable relation-ships have enhanced people's lives as the result of sports.

Sports bars all over the country are filled with the male species on any given night of the week depending on whether it's the playoffs, finals, championship, or just a game. For most people "the sports world" is a fantasy world; a place to get away to the sports bar or hide out in the "man cave". Men are drawn to sports like they are to the "great outdoors". Sports are exciting, adventurous, and there is true competition between muscled bodies using highly honed athletic skills in contests where there will be a winner. For many men, they are living the life of an athlete identifying with that spirit deep inside them through the television set.

Modern day sports are the result of men wanting their own male institution. The world of sports has come to symbolize the masculine structure of power over the feminization of society that began in the late 19th century. During the 1960's in the United States, activities like military sports were male building, masculine-identifying activities which set men apart from women. The acute interest in organized sport, mainly the big three, football, basketball, and baseball, have largely been played as a response to the over-feminization of men. Football is especially treasured as it is totally male dominated. It's an all guy sport that almost no woman is physically able to compete in; a legitimate way of keeping women at bay without incurring the hate of the "politically correct crowd" who know that in swimming and track women and men are fairly equal, but in sports that require strength, men are superior.

Boys and men want to know, "Can I take him?" Sport encourages boys to view other boys as rivals. Men who enter the world of sport come from all areas of life. They bring with them race, religion, class level, family structure, education level, ability, as well as mental stability. Freshmen enter college ready to conquer the world. While they are there to get an education, they are also there to play ball and to give every ounce of perspiration to the sports cause, but freshman underestimate how much of their conscious hours actually go into practice, traveling, practice, more traveling, and of course competition.

Lower class men see athletics as their ticket out of their "situation" and into the arena of public adulation and big bucks. During school, participation in athletics keeps the gangs at bay and brimgs admiration from peers. These men also see a commanding physique as a symbol of power and strength which equals toughness and garners respect. Many men from blue collar or the lower class do not visualize that playing sports would probably stop after high school when most player's "careers" come to an end. Playing professional sports is a dream for many, but there is a big difference between college and professional sports. Hours upon hours of practice will only lead some so far.

White middle class males, who emphasis education instead of sport, come to the conclusion that they have more choices. Middle class white men are more likely to have a backup plan to a sports career. They see an education as the ticket to their personal success. Often an athlete will come to the realization early and well before college, that professional sports is not the end goal. "Any man with a good trade is not about to get himself knocked on his butt to make a dollar". Strong family connections provide the framework upon which the athlete builds his choices. Men from a middle class background would describe their earliest athletic experience, motivation, and support directly related to their family who was their biggest fan. Nothing is as great as having a dad who is genuinely interested in their boy who is involved in sports.

Many boys join a sport for social reasons; to be part of the team. Some boys are pushed into sports by their fathers whether they have any interest or not. Gaining their father's approval was not to simply play but to play well. While some may resent this, others find out they are actually pretty good at their sport. Others feel like their fathers are living through them to relive their own athletic fantasies. One coach of a Little League team expected his son to be the star of the team.

Some athletes feel intimidated by accomplished older brothers or fathers. They want to be as good or better. It can be difficult to compete against "Dad the legend", his records, his trophies lining the school hallway, and the oft told stories of Dad the hero which have longed been ingrained into school lore. Schools now have TV's hanging in the gym hallway running former high school sports heroes. Pictures of Dad's accomplishments may still be hanging in the hallway staring you down every time you wander to PE reminding you of his hero status at one time.

Young men know that in the high school hierarchy anyone who has ever survived the teenage years without being permanently brain damaged knows the guys with the jerseys are at the top of the pecking order. Football is god in high school. The better the player the more he gets his picture in the paper, the better the player the more girls he gets, the better the player the more favors he gets. Not having natural ability, size, or interest in playing sports pretty much regulates the average kid to the bottom of the heap for the next four years. While a boy is enchanted with the idea of being on a team, being one of the guys, being number one, being recognized for his achievements, not all have the capabilities, size, talent, or interest for that matter. Many boys do not participate in sports.

There is certainly nothing unmasculine about playing in the band, participating on the debate team, or being involved in theater. (No one would suggest that Tom Hanks is not masculine.) A man is a man no matter the interest.

Boys and girls tend to play games differently. Girls will make exceptions in order to make the game fair. Boys are loyal to the rules. There are rules for a reason. Rules are concrete and they insure fairness. Rules are the safety net of contests and games. Girls would rather get along and be "fair".

Girls seem to be slowly creeping into the masculine world of sports. An 11-year-old girl goes to court so she has the right to play Little League with the boys. A high girl fights for her right to play quarterback on the high school football team. Girl on the high school wrestling team? How uncomfortable is that? Most boys would rather be dead than to be beat by a girl on the court, mat, or field. Defeat by a member of the female species means never living down that you have been officially "de-guyed".

The Augusta National Golf Club, where the Masters Golf tournament is played, was receiving some not so nice threats from a Ms. Martha Burke head of the National Council of Women's Organizations. She demanded that women be allowed entrance into this very private men's golf club. In order to join, a member had to be invited and the invitation did not include women. In this day of political correctness, there seemed to be only one choice for the club, but chairman "Hootie" Johnson's answer was absolutely NO. His response, "We will not be bullied, threatened, or intimidated. We do not intend to become a trophy in their display case. There may well become a day when women are invited to join our membership, but that timetable will be ours, and not at the point of a bayonet. Her threats mean nothing to me."

Meanwhile, the man was formulating a plan behind the curtain. As anyone knows, commercials keep tournaments in business and turning down the ladies' invitation to invite themselves into the men's club would most likely lead to sponsors pulling out in defense of the women. Plan B. Get only one sponsor. Not only was the Masters tournament a rousing hit (a record crowd tuned in to watch the commercial free competition) Ms. Burke hopped aboard her little pink golf cart and drove off into the proverbial sunset along with her clubs and empty threats. (Speaking facetiously of course.)

Teammates develop valuable and important relationships through sports, but professional sports are a business; a business where winning is what it is all about. Anyone who has fought his way to the top is constantly parrying those who want to knock him off and steal his job. It's about status. It's about money. It's about reputation. It's about winning, but worse of all, it's about a job. It is no longer a game. It's business.

In the U.S., football on television focuses mainly on those who carry, catch, throw, and kick the ball. The rest of the team is slamming their powerful bodies into each other. Football is a favorite although basketball is wildly popular. (Just ask any March Madness fan.) The sport has seen African Americans "put their stamp on the game of basketball" much to the pride of their community. Many key players in the league are African American and no one would argue that not only is Michael Jordan a fantastic player, but a gentlemen as well.

Athletes view their body as a machine. A well-tuned and well-oiled machine ready to be used at full capacity, but even a machine eventually breaks down. Drive by any "car graveyard" and you will notice a field littered with old school buses, pick-ups, and cool cars of the decade. The problem with viewing the body as a machine, is that the mind detaches from it allowing pain to become invisible, but the "machine" eventually falls apart and ends up in the "once was an athlete" graveyard.

Everyone is aware of the player who has the gift. They have what it takes, but when it comes to pulling it out, they clutch, freeze at "a crucial moment in a critical situation". They blow it. There's the guy who always seems to pull it off. Then there are men who play "through the pain" in between injections of painkillers. There are the guys who take steroids. The smaller guys may take steroids to keep up with larger guys who are knocking the crap out of them.

Anxious to get back into the game, many players have rushed their recovery only to find themselves reinjured. Injured players are avoided like the plague. Coaches cannot always tell who's faking it and who is really hurt, but either way he expects the athlete to suck it up and play through it which has the potential to leave a player crippled or in chronic pain for the rest of his life. Some guys are emotionally hurt being referred in female terms by his teammates when he refuses to play through the pain. The worst thing another player can do is to refer to his teammate as a _____. (Insert female term here.)

Basing personal value on how well you play the game and what the crowd and media think of you can totally deflate the ego leaving the athlete feeling valueless. An athlete's meaning and purpose has been derived from his athletic prowess. Call a man an ex-athlete is like calling him a girl. He feels his man status is immediately deflated when he no longer plays. Are you less of man if you decide that waking up as a cripple for the rest of your life is not for you because you decided to not "play through the pain"? NO. Your sports career is only a blip on your life's timeline. There are many more years ahead.

Sport does not always equate manliness with carrying a little brown ball down a field or stuffing a pumpkin-colored ball into a hoop. So what does it mean to be tough? Jockeys are some of the world's best athletes. For their size, horse jockeys are incredibly strong although they are not physically imposing. Pound for pound you won't find a stronger more athletic man than a horse jockey. For their size, jockeys are incredibly strong and are not padded from head to toe. Jockeys are required to weigh in between 100 and 127 pounds and are normally less than 5 feet 5 inches tall. These guys are controlling a 1000 pound animal .

Jockey insurance premiums remain among the highest in all professional sports. Injuries to the athlete may include concussion, bone fracture, arthritis, trampling, concussion, and paralysis. Horseracing is the only sport where an ambulance follows the athletes during the event. Often jockeys have to perform their job with very little compensation. In fact, about 75% of jockeys earn less than $40,000 per year and a horse falling on you is going to hurt a lot worse than 270 lb football player.

Sports from a History Perspective

At one time, football was a game of chance where players might meet their death and several did. President Theodore Roosevelt was concerned, after all, his own son played for Harvard. A meeting was set up to determine the fate of football. The year was October 1905. Members of the legislature were ready to make the game illegal if something didn't change, but legendary football coach John Heisman had an idea: legalize the forward pass, outlaw holding, and require the team to gain ten yards instead of five. This would eliminate major collisions. The new rules were adopted for the next season.

The "huddle" came about as the result of a deaf player who used sign language to talk to his fellow teammates. The huddle helped to keep his signals a secret. It was invented in 1894 by Gallaudet University. A deaf baseball player is the reason umpires adopted the "out", "safe", and "strike" signals.

While the United States holds football in high esteem, it cannot compete with soccer which is immensely popular throughout the world. The game of soccer can be traced back three thousand years. Baseball, basketball, and football don't even come close to the popularity of worldwide soccer. Soccer was a rousing hit in England at one time; the game engulfed entire towns who played against each other. Players would travel for miles shoving, pushing, grappling, and kicking as they ran across fields.

Soccer sounded like fun, but King Edward II didn't think so. In 1314, he had the Lord Mayor of London issue a royal proclamation banning the fun-loving, brawl-bashing, thud-crunching, ball game. According to King Edward's proclamation: "For as much as there is a great noise in the city caused by hustling over large balls, from er which many evils may arise, which God forbid, we command and forbid on behalf of the King, on pain of imprisonment". Other kings also felt like the rough game was keeping men from more important things like sharpening their archery skills which were needed to defend their country. Richard II and Henry IV also passed laws to ban soccer at the risk of a player being imprisoned. Elizabeth I herself tried to put a lid on "fute-ball". Unfazed by the royal's laws, the games continued. Henry VIII and Elizabeth I once again banned the sport, Elizabeth went as far as throwing disobeying players in the gaol (jail) for a week.

Germany, Japan, and China all played a version of the game of soccer in ancient times. In a match in ancient Rome,

2/3 of the sports team needed medical care after a particularly grueling contest which lasted fifty minutes. (Maybe the English kings had a point.)

And finally, America's pastime. As the story is rumored, Abner Doubleday invented baseball. Although it is doubtful that a Civil War hero, who had been in his grave for several years, could have had anything to do with the popular game. Baseball is based on a British sport called *rounders* that dates back to the mid 1700's.

Art Ingels came up with idea of go-karts when he built the first kart in 1956.

In1930, Hockey Goalie Abie Goldberry was smacked right in the pocket by a soaring puck which set him on fire. His teammates rushed to put him out. The puck had struck a package of matches he had in his pocket.

The chances of making two holes-in-one in the game of golf are 1 in 67 million.

It's a good thing we don't live in medieval times or you may have found yourself in the middle of a game of "hot cockles". The idea was to blindfold someone and whack him with a stick while he tried to guess who was administering each wallop.

Section IV

Bits and Thoughts

CHAPTER 9

FADS

C onfident people are self-assured because they are secure in who they are. Confidence does not always equal good looks, talent, athletic ability, or accomplishments. Confidence is an acceptance of who you are even if it means being different. Fads are not being different. People who are sucked into fads are usually going along with the group because "everyone's doing it".

Fads from this century include:

Flagpole Sitting - This fad became a popular spectator sport. It was started in 1920 by a professional stuntman who eventually set the world record for perching himself atop the pole for forty nine days.

Swallowing Goldfish became the thing to do in the 1930's. College students were especially into this tasty fin fad. (They were supposed to be the smart ones.) Makes you wonder how many beers it took to wash those little guys down. Harvard freshman and 1919 football captain Lothrop Withington Jr, bragged about how he had swallowed a goldfish once and was challenged to do it again for ten dollars which he naturally accepted. Pretty soon word got around about the feat and others were challenging the record and trying to one up each other declaring anyone that had swallowed less than the latest champ had guzzled down was a "sissy". Well, those were fighting words, of course. Before long, Albert Hayes at MIT, (remember, these were supposed to be the smart guys) downed 42 of the little gliders successfully. Joseph Deliberato slurped down 89 goldfish, which promoted the Massachusetts state legislature to introduce a bill for the protection of the golden swimmers. The bill would "preserve the fish from cruel and wanton consumption". Anyone caught snacking on the campus carp would be arrested. Besides, some goldfish carry tapeworms.

Hula Hoop In 1950, everyone seemed to have a hula hoop which was named after the Hawaiian dance. More than 25 million were sold only four months after it was introduced.

Telephone Booth Stuffing Packing your person with as many other people as humanly possible into a telephone booth in the 1950's was hugely popular. The stunt turned into a mathematical problem as many tried to figure out by using geometry and calculus how to fit as many people into the rectangular glass tube as possible.

Streaking The 70's meant tearing off shirts and skirts and running butt- naked across the football field or possibly an award show. While certainly eye-popping at first, like anything that is done to the point of exhaustion, people got used to seeing the hind end of the stark naked streaker and the fad soon faded.

TOGA! TOGA! TOGA! Anyone lucky enough to be alive in the 1970's hopefully got to experience this fad. Inspired by John Belushi in *Animal House,* Greek Toga parties became the thing to do. Wrapped only in a bed sheet, many college students attended these pseudo Roman parties. Going along with some fads isn't all bad even if you are dressed in a sheet.

Rubik's Cube   The Rubik's cube was a different story. A little brain power was needed to solve this puzzle which was originally invented by Emo Rubik as a mathematical tool to help his students with algebra. Fifty million were sold by 1980. Not bad.

Tattoos have taken over the current culture. "Sleeves" are every where. Everyone seems to have one, even the ladies who usually place the marking on the small of their back or ankle.

Mood Rings seemed to be on everyone's finger in the 1970's. If the ring turned black it meant you were upset. If the ring was blue you were happy, yellow tense, violet romantic. The crystals in the ring were sensitive to the body's temperature. Invented by Joshua Reynolds.

Pet Rocks We'll skip the pet rock. I'm sure the reader or anyone in their family didn't buy one of those. The pet rock was invented by Gary Dahl.

Glass Eating Professional linebacker for the Philadelphia Eagles Tim Rossovich decided to show anyone doubting his toughness how tough he really was. Snack of choice? Why, light bulbs of course. Not to be outdone, a Harvard man met the challenge by chomping on a globular bulb himself. Harvard decided that light bulb eating didn't fit into the curriculum anywhere and banned the practice.

Black Lights And speaking of bulbs, who didn't possess a room full of black lights as a teen in the 1970's. Black lights supposedly revealed hidden messages and symbols in posters as well as showing off one's pearly whites in the dark. T-shirts were also set aglow with one of these lights.

Troll Doll Thomas Dam created the "Dammit doll" or affectionately known by the masses as the troll doll. Invented for his daughter because he was short of cash, the bugged-eyed, big-haired little imp was inspired by stories of little creatures roaming the forest. Scandinavian myth dictates that trolls only appear at night because the sun will turn the creatures to stone.

Super Ball Zectron, no it's not the name of a some character from Star Wars, but a bouncy synthetic rubber which, when compressed into a ball, can bounce high into the air with one slam to the ground. Norman Stingley discovered the superball quite by accident.

Have A Nice Day   The Smiley Face is one of the most recognized faces. Little did H.R. Ball know that his symbol, which he never trademarked and was paid 45 dollars to create, would become an all time favorite used on zillions of items.

Sideburns These bushy-haired facial decorations became all the rage thanks to the King himself, Elvis Presley, but they were difficult to take care of and soon disappeared.

Duck Tail Was worn by only the cool guys affectionately known as greasers. Hair was combed back on either side and then flipped into a tail in the back and held together by hair grease.

Sea Monkeys Many kids checked their mailbox everyday in the 1960's while they waited for a box of Sea Monkeys to arrive. The package often showed mom and dad with their cute little Sea Monkey kids on the box. What they actually were was Artema nyos, a creature related to the brine shrimp. They could survive outside of water, but quickly came to life when placed back into the water. Harold von Braunhut discovered the oddity in 1957 and as they say, the rest is history.

Cigars It's a good thing the politically correct crowd wasn't around in the state of Iowa way back when or children would not have been able to enjoy favorite treats which included bubble gum cigars and Blackjack chewing gum. (A smoking ban has been passed in the corn state.)

<u>Panty Raids</u> With the never-ending exposure of the younger generation's skivvies, panty raids seem amusingly archaic, but they were fun at the time. Started at the University of Michigan in 1952, colleges all over the country soon followed suit by invading and rescuing women's lingerie from the girls' dorm rooms.

<u>Latest fad</u> Japanese farmers have invented the square watermelon. They say it stacks better. They are grown in square tempered glass cases and resemble large Christmas candles.

A tip of the hat to the inventors of these fads, while a few are surrounded in mystery as to how they came about, the rest were invented by men. Fads are just that, fads. Ideas that blow in as fast they fizzle out. While many last for only a short term, the guys who came up with them are laughing all the way to the bank.

Never underestimate first year sales of new products. The VW Beetle only sold 330 cars and Coca-Cola sold only 25 bottles of their tasty carbonated thirst quencher the first year.

CHAPTER 10

BEER SAVES THE
DAY AND OTHER SUCH NONSENSE

Vlad the Impaler ruled an area called Walachia which is modern day Romania. He ruled with an iron hand and had no mercy for those who disobeyed him. The ruler impaled people by the thousands and sometimes washed down his meals with their blood. He is said to have skinned unfaithful lovers alive. When two visiting ambassadors refused to remove their hats saying it was not the custom in their country, Vlad had their hats nailed to their heads. His life inspired Bram Stoker to create his character Dracula. Vlad's father was known as Dracula.

BEER SAVES THE DAY! The Mayflower was on path for Virginia when storms blew it off course causing the ship to crash against the shore of Massachusetts. Seeing how they were running low of a certain adult beverage, the passengers decided to dock at Plymouth Rock, their "victuals were much spent". Since the beer barrels were dry, a brew house was erected. In those days, beer was considered an essential and healthy part of the daily meal. Water was considered suspect because it was easily contaminated with disease. Queen Elizabeth I's favorite beverage was beer.

ENGLISHMAN WORKS TO ABOLISH SLAVERY John Newton started the slave trade at age 20 and eventually worked his way up to captain of his own slave ship. On one unusually savage day, his ship found itself floundering on the sea during a rousing storm. The blustery winds grabbed hold of the ship tossing it about like a toy boat and threatened to capsize his vessel. "God have mercy!" begged Newton and the waves died down. Until then Newton had never been a religious man and the moment changed his life forever. Newton left the slave trade and began crusading against slavery. So moved by the presence of God's forgiving love that he was inspired to write one of the most loved and cherished hymns of all time, "Amazing Grace". He lived long enough to see the slave trade abolished.

CHAPPE INVENTS MECHANICAL INTERNET During the 1790's, dozens of odd looking towers sprang up all across France like June bugs on a hot night. The towers were the brainchild of Claude Chappe. Each one had mechanical arms that rotated in many different combinations and were visible as far as ten miles away. An operator would set the arms in a certain position then the operater in the next tower would see them through a telescope so he could set his arms in the same way. Impressed, Napoleon ordered new lines built from Paris to be set in every direction. Five hundred towers were erected and other countries followed suit. The invention of the electrical telegraph made the Chappe telegraph obsolete. Today only a few hundred of the towers remain.

HE WANTS YOU Sam Wilson had a contract to supply meat to US troops during the war of 1812. The meat was shipped with "U.S." stamped on the barrels. The abbreviation wasn't as common as it is today and many people were curious as to what U.S. stood for. Why, it was for "Uncle Sam" Wilson, the meat packer's nickname. People loved it and before you knew it, it became the country's nickname. There were several drawings of Uncle Sam, but the one that stuck was painted by artist James Montgomery Flagg; an image forever immortalized in a WWI poster. It showed a stern fellow with a goatee and a red, white, and blue outfit pointing his finger at potential recruits.

JUST WHISTELING DIXIE "Dixie", the anthem of the south was actually written in New York by a Yankee, a man from Ohio. The year was 1859. In 1861, after the inauguration of Jefferson Davis as president of the confederate States of America, the jaunty tune became the marching song of the Confederate Army. This was an outrage to Daniel Decatur Emmet who was a staunch Union supporter. "I'll be damned when I'd written it if I knew what they were going to do to my song," Emmet declared.

PRIVATE EYE Sherlock Holmes is based on Dr. Joseph Bell, a professor of medicine at the University of Edinburgh. One of Bell's students was so impressed by the man's amazing ability of observation that he called it Bell's "eerie trick of spotting details". Bell seemed to be able to determine what his patients did for a living by watching them walk or just by looking at a patient, then diagnosing the problem. His keen powers of observation forever sealed his place in history as a pioneer in forensic science. The student, who began to write stories of the famous detective Sherlock Holmes based on his perceptive teacher, was Arthur Conan Doyle.

CORNFLAKES John Harvey Kellogg was a medical doctor in Battle Creek Michigan and the new fitness guru of the time. He strongly believed the key to happiness lay in the digestive tract. Kellogg was a devoted vegetarian and did not drink or smoke. He was convinced that indigestion was responsible for more deaths than all other causes combined.

John, and his brother Will Keith Kellogg, began producing whole grain cereals. The boys had a disagreement, however, over what ingredients to put in their newfound discovery to enhance their new addition to the breakfast table. Will went off and created The Battle Creek Toasted Corn Flake Company so he could add sugar to his cereal recipes, a concept that John, who was a health freak, would not tolerate.

Aside from sibling rivalry, John and Will were marketing geniuses. In a famous add, the Kellogg boys asked buyers not to purchase their cereal because of a shortage. Asking someone not to do something often produces the opposite affect which it did in this case. People flocked to the stores to buy their cereal.

EVEREADY Joshua L. Cowen had a passion for railroads. He was an inventor who designed many things. Among the many ideas he came up with were little metal tubes called dry cell batteries. Eventually he grew bored of the invention and gave it away to one of his salesmen. As any clever dealer who came across a million dollar idea would do, the salesman ran with the idea and named his company American Eveready Company. Next, Cowen designed a tiny electric motor for a miniature fan. It was just the right size to power a mini train. He started selling them and customers fell in love with the motorized models and begun buying them for Christmas gifts for their children. The L in the middle stands for Lionel. Lionel trains.

YOU'RE OUT! The origins of American baseball is said to be invented by an American Civil War hero by the name of General Abner Doubleday, a report that was supported by A. G. Spalding. Doubleday was14 years in the grave before there was even a faint hint that he had created baseball. A well known British sport called *rounders* was surprisingly similar to the new American pastime.

RACE ACROSS ALASKA In January of 1925 a diphtheria epidemic broke out among the children of Nome, Alaska. The nearest life saving serum was in Anchorage 700 miles away. The decision was made to mush the serum to the sick children by dogsled teams from Anchorage. " Wild Bill Shannon" was the first man who would carry the serum. Along the way, the temperature reached a bone-chilling 40 below with blinding snow and ferocious winds. On the fifth day, Gunnar Kaassen and his lead dog Balto, delivered the serum arriving 5 ½ days later short of 5:00 a.m. The trip inspired the Iditarod which is held in Alaska every March between Anchorage and Nome.

SMALL POX BIG IDEA Small pox is an infectious disease which has caused death to millions of people worldwide. In 1796, Edward Jenner, a British scientist, first inoculated a boy from small pox when he discovered a person could retain immunity by being inoculated using cowpox vesicles.

D DAY INVASION A New Orleans boat builder by the name of Andrew Jackson Higgins had a hard time convincing the Navy to try his boats which were built out of wood, but eventually won them over. He developed and built landing craft used for the Normandy Invasion. During the D- day invasion of June 1944, more than 150,000 soldiers stormed the beaches of Normandy safely due to one man named Andrew Jackson Higgins. He was also a mass production genius and was able to turn out 20,000 landing craft which, according to General Eisenhower, is what won WWII.

JUST LIKE MAGIC For those single bachelors who couldn't make it without their microwave, they have Percy Spencer to thank. While working at the Raytheon Company Percy discovered a more efficient way to manufacture magnetrons, which are "high-powered vacuum tubes that generate coherent micro-waves".Standing in front of the magnetron one day, he felt a gooey mess in his pocket. His chocolate candy bar had melted which prompted him to wonder if the magnetron could be responsible. He then placed corn kennels in front of it and they popped. The microwave was born. The earliest model weighed 750 pounds and cost 3000 dollars. Today you can pick one up for as cheap as 40 dollars.

T.I.M. (NOT THE TOOLMAN) Anyone who has a computer is familiar with www.com, but exactly how did the world wide web come about? In 1980, a man by the name of Tim Berners-Lee, a soft ware consultant, came up with a clever way to organize his notes. He designed software that would take all his information and allow him to access it through links. The idea next was to link information from one computer to another.

The "www" was first called "the mesh" and the "The Information Mine" which was thrown out because the first letters were TIM which sounded a bit pompous. His friends called it "that hypertext thing", but World Wide Web sounded better. Interestingly both parents were mathematicians who built one of the earliest computers.

GATORADE Developed at the University of Florida and named after the Florida Gators is a delicious drink that replaces lost fluids and electrolytes in the players. It worked! The Gators started winning games like crazy.

CHAPTER 11

Just A Thought

Male intuition is not an oxymoron. Have you ever had a feeling about that something just didn't feel right? Or that someone was poking around in your house, car, or desk that should not have been there? But you have no proof? Sometimes we understand things without knowing why we do. It's intuition and yes, guys have it to. You don't like a particular person, but can't quite say why. You would rather skip a specific meeting. You know it would never work with the girl everyone is always trying to set you up with. Sometimes we just get it. We just know. Sometimes the so-called quick decision can be as good as the long drawn one that you have contemplated for days or weeks. Why? Because there are times when we can look at a situation and accurately size it up quickly without thinking it to death.

One person has known since kindergarten he was going to marry a particular girl, did, and was successful at it. Another person drags the dating process on for 6 years before marrying the person and it does not work out. One man who knew a girl for only three weeks has been married to his sweetheart for 25 years. A college student dates a girl all through college and still can't make up his mind. Each man probably knew soon after meeting the person whether she was the right one. Any woman that has to cajole her long time boyfriend into marrying her is asking for a problem. He has not married her for a reason. He has already assessed the relationship and knows whether it will work or not. Meanwhile, why not date her if she's cute?

The ability to "thinslice" as author Malcolm Gladwell refers to it, is the ability of our subconscious to find patterns in situations and behaviors based on very narrow slices of experience. We are able to sum up something sometimes very quickly based on an instant analysis of something. For example, there are times when a police officer looks at a situation and senses that something "just isn't right". He is not quite sure what it is, but something doesn't look right. He is able to hone in a something subtle, something seemingly insignificant. The practice of inferring the motivations and intentions of others, of sizing up a situation within seconds, of instinctively knowing something is right or not right is classic thin slicing.

Have you ever watched the face of a baby when he looks at another baby and that baby starts to cry? A happy baby can go straight to the tears after seeing the face of another unhappy baby. Faces are infectious. Voluntary expression is the way we intentionally single our emotions, but the faces we make without thinking about them are genuine faces. We relay to the world how we really feel. A grumpy mug can immediately upset the person next to him. Babies and handicapped people cannot fake expressions. They are sad or happy or mad. One of the things that is so endearing about babies is that they are real.

The media is an example of sensory overload. A glut of too much information can be intimidating as well as excessive. Do we really need to see a video of the latest school shooting at every angle possible with every analyst scrutinizing it with a razor sharp tongue? Sometimes one glance is all someone needs to size up the situation if it is presented honestly. The first few seconds of a video of a gang beating of an innocent high school girl is enough. We are instantly disgusted by the sight. We know it is wrong. We know it is vile. We know "nice" adolescents do no climb out of closets and pummel someone into uncon-sciousness. We do not need to analyze a vicious beating until it becomes nothing more than a casual smack. There are times when scrutinizing an event, speech, or person puts the brain into overload. A guy can come to a conclusion based on instinct; his first impression of something as well as making a conscious decision by weighing the facts in a thoughtful way.

Autistic people cannot read faces. They tend to see people as just another object in the room. They are not able to pick up on nonverbal cues or facial expressions. Many autistic people avoid eye contact. This critical point has enormous implications for the art of mind reading and being able to assess a situation. Micro expression is a critical kind of facial expression. It's often made without thought in a split second. That's why even though someone may be smiling we might ask the person why they are mad, or if something is wrong. Often some little part of a suppressed emotion leaks out. We are not always aware of our expression.

Upon closer observation, a viewer can tell what the politician is really thinking. True emotions cannot be tailored behind a frozen smile. Your face reflects what is going on in your mind. Politicians, with their department store mannequin poses and smiles, will signal their real feelings to another human if he is paying attention. You may not be able to state what it is about someone that appears insincere, or that they he is lying, but it comes through even though it is hidden behind promises and hundred dollar words:

Sizing it up. Don't you love the word "rightsizing"? Less money for more work.

Plan B According to James York, the most successful people are those who are good at plan B.

How to make a sale A good salesman realizes that everyone is a potential customer. You cannot prejudge. You have to be willing to give everyone your best shot. You don't know who is a "cash buyer" or just a window shopper. Women do not necessarily mean nonbuyers. Many women make a higher salary than men and they are fully capable of purchasing a car, a house, or stocks on their own. After all, she was able to pass the medical boards, get her real estate license, or graduate with a four year degree. Do not judge a buyer based on their appearance!

Men are literally strangling themselves 12% of men's ties are too tight, tight enough to restrict blood flow to the old noodle.

Tallness does not equal leader Everyone has an idea of what a leader is supposed to look like. Many times George W. Bush walked several feet apart from the former president of Mexico Vicente Fox who was a towering 6' 5" to Bush's 5'11". Tallness is equated with leadership and authority. That's unfortunate because IQ points do not add up with extra inches. The American Express CEO is 5'9" and black. There are exceptions.

The Committee is in Rarely does the group make profound decisions. Can you imagine several generals and other high-ranking officers calling a time out during battle, pulling out their clipboards and notes, and discussing what should be done next? People in positions of leadership are generally there because they make decisions well and when someone's life depends on it. Those decisions can be on the battlefield or in the hospital room and they can be the difference between life and death. People such as firefighters, doctors, nurses, and soldiers are people who can make decisions under pressure. Good decisions are not made by committees.

The Crystal Ball What sets good decision makers apart from people who make poor decisions is the ability to foresee the future. True wisdom only comes from a lifetime, but good decision making can come at any age. Your decisions impact every area of your life. Sometimes for the rest of your life. Is she really so hot that 20 minutes of fun is worth 18 years of child support payments? Is taking the first job that pays 10 dollars an hour after high school the way to go? Will you still be happy with that 10 dollars in 10 years? Is it a better deal than going to college or trade school? Or auto mechanic school? Or any school for that matter where you can begin a foundation to set the building of your future on? Do you really have to have that SUV? Now? Are you going to be happy with it six years from now when you are still forking over 600 a month of your salary for a set of wheels that depreciated 3000 dollars when you drove it off the lot? And put you upside down if you trade it in?

Does everyone really need to go to college? NO! But no one wants to be stuck on the barely-able-to-buy groceries salary. Good decision makers balance the future with where they are today. Good decision makers are able to postpone the desires of today for the security of tomorrow. Making decisions at one time took careful thought and consideration. Now people expect an important decision along with their delivered pizza. Because we are surrounded by instant communication, others expect immediate action NOW. Decisions require more than the tapping of buttons. Decisions require thought.

Fight or flight What happens to a person when they become hyper-aroused? He shuts down. Have you ever tried to argue with a raging person? Not only is it not possible, but probably not a good idea either. The person has literally shut off and zoned out.

Emergency situations also tend to do this to the average person. Once the heart reaches 145 beats per minute, the person is in trouble. Motor skills break down and at 175 beats per minute, we literally become a tub of goo. That is why dialing something as simple as 911 all of sudden seems overwhelming. Our senses and ability to reason collapse. In extremely stressful situations, a person will lose control of their bowels. The body literally shuts down all necessary functions with our blood pooling form the outer layers of muscle to the core muscle mass.

The muscle turns hard to prevent massive bleeding. This why we feel like a jelly fish when an emergency hits.

The Police   Most police cars are no longer stocked with two officers. While the average person might think that doesn't sound like a good idea, it has been discovered that pairing two policeman together gives them a false sense of boldness. A lone officer is not nearly as quick to jump into a risky situation. He will think before acting. Officers in numbers produce a false sense of "bravado". They think they can tackle whatever comes their way. The same thing happens with a group of men or boys. Suddenly they are all tough guys.

Collision of the worlds An episode of *Seinfeld* has George Costanza with his underwear in a knot over the supposed "collision of his worlds". He preferred to keep certain people in each of his special worlds and not mix his friends and acquaintances. In reality, the more worlds you occupy the more powerful you are; the broader your network. A person who is a doctor will know many people in the medical field, but if that doctor participates in community plays, he now is exposed to the artsy group and their friends. Let's say the doctor is part owner in a small restaurant. He is exposed to people in the restaurant business as well as the variety of customers who come to eat there. Occupying several worlds exposes a person to many opportunities that would not exist if he remained in the same profession, same neighborhood, or same clubs with the same people.

When it comes to finding new jobs, new information, or new ideas, weak ties are always more important than strong ties. Your friends occupy the same world as you do. Your acquaintances occupy an entirely different world. Weak ties are people who run with different crowds and people not in the same profession as you; the people you run with, eat at the same places with and work out at the same places with. People in other worlds have different ties and sometimes know of possible jobs, or opportunities that you would not otherwise come across. Did you know that 56 % of people found their jobs through personal connections 18% used formal means like advertisements or headhunters and 20 percent applied directly?

Mass Communicatin' In this day and age of "mass communicatin" as Pappy O'Daniel calls it, a social bird's opinion of the last restaurant he ate at, or latest movie he went to, the last house or neighborhood he lived in, the last company he worked for, or the last school his kids went to or the latest hotel he stayed in has weight. A particular professor, client, customer, neighbor, or a likable fellow can have a lot of influence on the rest of us. Connectors are the people who know lots of people. They are the people who occupy many different worlds, subcultures, and niches. With the over advertizination of our society (is that a word?) word of mouth is as important as ever. A respected or well-liked person's opinion of something carries tremendous weight.

The Midnight Ride of Paul Revere Paul Revere was very social and talkative. When he died, his funeral was attended by "troops of people". He was active in many clubs and a successful businessman. He was always at the center of events. Paul Revere became more and more convinced as he observed the Boston harbor that the British were about to make a major move. There was a little too much activity going on. He jumped on a horse and began his midnight ride to Lexington. In just 2 hours, he covered 13 miles. In every town he passed through he knocked on doors and spread the word telling the local colonial leaders that the "British are coming!" "The British are coming!" Church bells rang and drums started to beat. The same time Revere was beginning his journey, William Dawes was on his way to warn the colonists. So why haven't we heard about this fellow? Revere had an array of social gifts and knew lots of people. Paul Revere was one of those people that everyone knew.

When the redcoats began their march toward Lexington on the 19th of April 1775 they were met with resistance much to their surprise. There were no cell phones, text messaging, Tweets, e-mail alerts, or news bulletins. The warning was given purely through word of mouth and maybe a little shouting, too. Two men: William Dawes and Paul Revere. Both galloping wildly through the night their capes flapping madly in the cloak of darkness spreading the news that the British were on the way, yet we don't sing little ditties about Dawes and there is no 60's band called William Dawes and the Raiders.

Media overload E-mail used to be exciting stuff. It is a quick way of contacting someone and knowing that the person will likely get the message. But now e-mail has been hijacked by advertisements, psychics, male enhancement products, guys from Nigeria, and solicitations that no human being should be subjected to. The virtual space is now the junk zone. The E-mail zone has become a dumping ground for every investment scam. It is a routine part of many people's day to flip through the mail and delete junk as fast as their mouse can scurry across the screen.

Baseball the American pastime The perimeter of the baseball field is splattered with advertisements for local restaurants or a picture of the grinning local newscast. Even the names of fields are advertisements for businesses. Why would anyone want to read the junk surrounding the field when you can watch kids dressed as hotdogs racing around the field for a t-shirt? Now, there's real entertainment.

Building blocks Connectors are the little pieces in an erector set Legos, or K'nex building toys. They are the hinges, the snaps, the corner end pieces of the set that bond all the other pieces together. Without them, the structure would collapse. Connecting people are like that. They are the link between new acquaintances, business associates, possible friends, future mates, and business deals. Their social ability is the glue that brings new people together. This person knows many people who knows many people who knows some people who knows others. This person has secured jobs for others through faint acquaintances, recommended the best place to stay while you are on your vacation, suggested the finest restaurant in town to eat, and offered insight on who to buy a car from. Get to know a connecter. He is a valuable person to have in your people collection.

Silence is golden One of the biggest problems people have while engaging in conversation is overspeaking. Breaking in to talk over someone before the other guy has finished his thought is one of the most irritating things about news commentary or talk shows. No one gets a chance to finish a sentence before someone else busts in and interrupts. In modern journalism you see the over exaggeration of head movements, gestures, pronunciation of words, and snarky fake concern when they are relaying a news story. They are so wrapped up in the sound of their own voice and, unfortunately today, their opinion, which should not even be a part of the news story.

Most people like to talk about themselves (even news people) and they want to be listened to when they are talking about themselves. The ability to stay put and really hone in on what someone is saying to you will not only make you a better doctor, sales person, restaurant owner, or delivery person, it might possibly make you a new friend which translates into a new client or contact.

What is it? *It* is what we call charisma; the ability to inspire enthusiasm, interest, or affection in others by means of personal charm or influence. We pick up miniscule cues from a speaker, but altogether they relay a message. Does the speaker like what he is talking about? Is he bored with it? Are his points well made? If he is running for office, would you vote for him? A relaxed pleasant face, looking into someone's eyes and not interrupting, and nodding your head at appropriate intervals tells the speaker you are paying attention.

Play nice Why do we go to the same restaurants? Because we like the food? Why do we enjoy having the same person cut our hair? Why do we request a certain doctor? Why do we hope our child will get that special teacher? Why do we have favorite radio personalities we like to listen to? Because they are kind, treat us with a special flair, make us feel like we are worth their time, ask us how we are and really mean it, treat us like the best audience anyone could ever have. Nice people make us feel like we are valuable.

School does no determine who you will be Anyone who has ever taught school for more than a year has no doubt come across a student who, well, puzzled them. They know the child is intelligent, that he or she shows talent in certain areas, but the child tested poorly. Take the case of a boy who is now 20 years old. His test scores were so low that one would have thought he had the IQ of a radish. There was great concern over this boy. Meetings were set up, special classes were offered and concern over whether or not he would ever have any chance in life was tossed around. It is probably safe to say that 99% of his teachers based their opinion of this young man solely on test scores.

Can you test uniqueness? Can you test someone who has the ability to play any tune on the piano by ear? Can you test a person who can paint or draw? Or create exquisite meals? The ability to memorize lots of unnecessary junk and test well on it is, well, the ability to memorize lots of unnecessary junk and test well on it. Just as the ability to draw well, the ability to understand complicated math problems, the ability to run a restaurant and create fabulous meals, the ability to understand mechanical systems, the ability to understand and work with animals, and the ability to throw a ball farther than anyone else. These are all gifts. Yet, the only ability that is tested in the school is the one where you are able to memorize lots of information. So much is placed on the "test" and that's great if you are a test taker. Some people are not.

Did you ever feel really dumb in school because you couldn't take a quiz no matter how much you studied? Were you often told that you weren't trying hard enough? Or you were lazy? Maybe you were told that you just weren't motivated and if you only tried a little harder…Things like persistence, attitude, motivation, desire, being able to set and follow through on goals, and personal vision cannot be measured or tested.

The late ABC News anchor Peter Jennings, actor/comedian Chris Rock, and TV Judge Greg Mathis all have something in common. None of them finished high school and all earned their GED. Don't let school define you. Jennings was a high school dropout. Judge Mathis was born in Detroit where he lived in a housing project. With three older brothers who were involved in criminal activity, he soon followed. He became involved in using and selling drugs, stealing, and even shot at the police one time. His father was a member of a gang and young Greg ended up with the street gang the Errol Flynns. While he was a teenager sitting in jail, his mother came to visit him. He had reached the point where he could have headed further into the wrong direction. Mathis loved his mother and news that she had colon cancer was devastating to him as she had always tried her best to model a decent life for her boys. Upon his release from jail, he was given probation with the stipulation that he would maintain a full time job at McDonalds. And from there, he decided to head down a different path.

A reputation is priceless "Confession is good for the soul but bad for the reputation". Be careful what you say and to whom you say it to.

Check is in the mail Some people sit around waiting for the government fairy Godmother to show up at their door with a check. A lot of people act like life owes them, the government owes them, the boss owes them, the wife owes them. Owed what? You can't be your own man when you walk around with your hand out. Don't be the guy standing at the door of success not bold enough to knock and go in.

You never know when your time is up Attila the Hun, King of the Huns, commanded an army of half a million men for 20 years. Did he succumb to an arrow piercing his heart? Was he captured and tortured by his enemy? Did an accident claim him or did he succumb to starvation? After marrying and enjoying his wedding ceremony, he fell into a drunken sleep and developed a nosebleed. The fiercest of warriors was known to have chronic nosebleeds which caused him to choke to death.

The American Dream Very few things are as invigorating as traveling the road of life armed with a sense of direction towards a goal. If you want something badly enough you can do anything if you are willing to pay the price, but driven people often find success at the price of their family. When they arrive at the diamond door of success, they realize they are not any happier. It is the joy of pursuing the goal that triumphs obtaining it. Sure, people admire and envy the moppy-haired titans who have "made it", but at what price?

No one does it alone 'Success is the point at which preparation meets opportunity". Success never just happens. Behind every successful individual is someone else. Be generous and give credit where credit is do.

Be forgiving of others As Henry Wadsworth Longfellow once stated, "If we could read the secret history of our enemies, we should find in each man's life sorrow and suffering enough to disarm all hostility".

There's more to life than running across a pretty green field for 45 million dollars a year and a chance to have your face plastered on the latest cereal box.

Posers Everyone knows one, but toughness comes in all packages. Genghis Khan, literally means "universal ruler". The Mongolian conqueror was 5'1" inches tall, yet greatly feared. Born in 1162, he tore through Asia, the Middle East, and Europe. Genghis Khan was the grandfather of another famous ruler, Kublai Khan. Few would argue that Khan was not a man to be reckoned with.

Napoleon Bonaparte was known as "The Little Corporal". He was a French ruler and leader who was 5' ft 2" inches tall. Born in Ajaccio, Corsica Napoleon was considered a military genius and highly successful military leader. No poser here. According to sources, at his death he had grown to the amazing height of 5'6".

Morihei Ueshiba was born December 14, 1883. He was a famous martial artist and founder of the Japanese martial art of Aikido. Morihei was 5'ft 2" inches tall. Real men come in all sizes.

CHAPTER 12
CHOOSING
THE RIGHT ADULT BEVERAGE

If it tastes like pop with added alcohol it is not a great beer: it is a means of delivering alcohol to the brain without the intervention of taste. Great beers have great taste, aroma, texture, flavor, and a nice finish or "after taste". This according to a renowned beer expert and connoisseur. That's the point isn't it? The alcohol to the brain part.

Bud, Miller, and Coors adult beverages are based on a pilsner beer from Czechoslovakia which are modified lager beers. All are an American lager which is a style of pilsner. They are golden light beers which deliver a clean crisp flavor. The terms lager and pilsner are used interchangeably. Europeans tend to be a little snooty when it comes to these beers finding them tasteless.

What does it say about a man who likes something a little different? Something, like say, a hardy stout? The guys who drink these beers are connoisseurs. They know a good beer from a bad beer. They care whether it tastes good or not. They care if it delivers the "great taste, aroma, texture, flavor, and nice finish".

Beer is actually divided into two groups: Lagers and Ales. Ninety five percent of beers are pilsner. Pilsner beer originated in the town of Pilsen (Plzen), which at one time, was in Bohemia, but is now the Czech Republic. It was first brewed in 1842 and quickly became a hit. It is the most popular style of beer in the world. The color of this adult lubricant depends on what is being used to make it; the type of malt and hops. The beverage comes in various shades of browns and golds; some resemble the color of mud. Beer drinkers sometimes think that darker richer beers are more alcoholic.

According to several different sources, the best beer in the world is Westvleteren 12 brewed by Westvleteren Abdj St. Sixtus in Belgium. It is a dark, cloudy brown beer brewed mostly under the care of monks. Good luck getting a case of this beer.

Each type of beer is fermented differently: lagers in cold temperatures, ales in warm temperatures. Lager flavor comes from barley and hops. With ales you will get slight fruit flavors like peach apricot. If you drink imports you will get drunk faster than with domestic beers.

Although beers, bars, and sports go together, some brewskies are savored by true beer aficionados who relish every drop. There is no rule that you have to order a "specialty drink" because you are in a bar. It is perfectly acceptable to order a beer. Picking the right adult beverage on a first date will say something about you and your date. Fruity numbers topped with cute, colorful umbrellas, ice cream concoctions you need a straw to drink with, and "tini" numbers (fruity martini drinks) are best left to your date. Your best bet is to probably stick with beer. After all, you are probably comfortable with the familiar brew.

If you are a light beer drinker, it singles that you are watching your waistline. Seriously? Do men do that? Nah. Or maybe you are not really a beer drinker and don't really care what the beverage tastes like. Are you a risk taker? A specialty beer is probably for you. Micro breweries have popped up everywhere. You're taking a chance with a craft beer, but what the heck, you might find something that inspires your taste buds.

"Session" beer is a term for low alcohol beer that you will probably be nursing all night. Beer does not have to match the food you order. Mainstream beer is perfectly agreeable to have with your dinner. Some wine and food combinations don't work such as wine and Asian cuisine. Porterhouse beer goes great with a porter house steak. They are both hardy.

Many people associate beer with sports bars, back yard barbecues, and baseball games. Some drink it as a thirst quencher after an exhausting day of work. What makes the golden pilsners so appealing is the fact they can be drunk with almost any meal, especially pizza. Fruit beers go well with barbecues.

Types of beer:

Ale : English language term for beer made by water fermentation

Lager : beer fermented and matures at low temperatures

Pilsner: golden lager

Stout: dark brown to black: made with highly roasted grains

Many of the world's best known beers are almost tasteless according to beer experts.

Wine

The word wine comes from the Old English word *"win"* which can be traced back to the Latin word *vinum* meaning "vine". Sixty million-year-old fossil vines have been discovered. The roots (no pun intended) of this delicious palate-inspiring beverage can be traced back 7,000 to 8,000 years to Georgia on the Black Sea. The story of wine is rich in history. The history of wine and people go back thousands of years.

Wine has been and is still a part of many functions. The Egyptians left detailed pictures in tomb paintings of the art of winemaking. The Greek's god of wine is Dionysus while the Romans looked to the god of wine, Bacchus. The use of wine is associated with religious ceremonies such as Communion in Christianity. At one time, wine was used as a medicine. It was also a crash crop for some. In 1922, British archaeologists Howard Carter and Lord Carnarvon discovered a young Egyptian king's tomb. King Tutankhamen was an Egyptian Pharaoh who ruled between 1333 B.C.-1322 B.C. and whose rule was cut short either by murder or accident. He was only 19-years-old when he died. In his tomb many treasures were discovered. One of the most intriguing discoveries were jars of wine with the year, winemaker, and notes pertaining to the quality of the beverage, but it is doubtful that they would have placed bad wine in a King's tomb!

During medieval times, wine was stored in barrels. Not a drop was wasted even after it turned to vinegar. Thomas Jefferson, third president of these United States of America, was a wine connoisseur and traveled to Europe to bring back the best of wines.

Wine has truly stood the test of time. It has been enjoyed by people from all over the world for thousands of years. People associate wine with classiness and ceremony. It's a special beverage that people use to celebrate special occasions. Although European and North American wine is made from fermented grapes, wine can also be made out of rice, fruit, and vegetables. Viking Leif the Lucky, upon his discovery of America, named it Vinland for all the grapevines he observed when he landed in the area of what is now New York although California produces about 90% of the wine in the United States today.

Wines can be red, white, or blush. Temperature and region play a part in the character of wine; color, palate, and body. There are three types of wine: Dry, Sweet, and Sparkling are all made in red or white varieties of grapes. Dry wines are light wines with very little sugar added and are considered healthful.

Sweet wines have the addition of grape brandy. It is much sweeter than a dry wine. Sweet wines are used as medicinal wines, after dinner drinks, and for cooking purposes. Sparkling wines are fermented twice. The second fermentation produces carbonic gas which produces the glittering dancing bubbles that promotes celebrations.

You can't go wrong ordering a nice glass of wine with dinner .A glass of wine is a good beverage to start out with. Red wine goes well with many meals. Red wines use red or black grapes and good quality red wines improve in flavor with age when properly stored. If you or your date are partial to different wines, it best for each person to order a glass instead of a bottle. Zinfandel sweet wines are for women. White wines are made mostly with white grapes although light flesh colored red grapes will sometimes be used. Popular white wines include Chardonnay, Sauvignon Blanc, Chenin Blanc, and Pinot Blanc. You might look stupid walking around with a wine glass while everyone else is drinking a beer or vice versa.

"Vintage" wine sounds expensive and it can be. Vintage wine is a good wine made in a certain region from a particular harvest of grapes in a specified year. The wine is good by itself and does not have to be blended with other wine to make it taste better. Most countries allow a vintage wine to include a small portion of wine that is not from the labeled vintage. Vintage does not necessarily mean an old wine bottle covered with dust or cobwebs. What makes it costly is that the wine is made from a particular harvest of grapes and then bottled from one batch. This ensures that all the bottles from that year will taste relatively the same. People who know their way around wine will hang on to an especially good vintage for a special occasion. Whereas "non vintage" wine blends wines from two or more years which gives a consistency and predictability to a particular style of wine year after year.

It is nearly impossible to produce the same bottle of wine. So many things go into making wine: the weather and the grapes to name a few. Anything exquisite and appealing to the human being will either encompass hard work, persistence, time, or money. Producing a great wine is no exception. It takes expertise, love of the wine making process, and money to produce an outstanding product.

The majority of people purchase wine at the grocery store. How much should you pay for wine? It really depends on what you are going to celebrate. A person would probably not buy the stuff we got looped on as teenagers. Hopefully we are at a place now where we are able to afford something a little bit better.

Red wines are best served slightly cooler than room temperature. Many people see red wine as a sophisticated addition, yet some people get headaches or migraines from drinking red wine. Store sparkling dry white wines and sweet wines in the refrigerator for about an hour before serving.

You can tell real wine drinkers by the way they hold their glass. Don't assume that you are the only one that is wine illiterate. Blush and Zinfandel wines are usually ordered by people who are not regular wine drinkers and who are not connoisseurs of what constitutes an excellent wine. If your date orders a white wine, she probably is not much of a drinker. Also the blush wines are for folks who don't know one end of a wine bottle over another. These wines just taste good.

Always serve sparkling wine in tall narrow flutes. Helps keep those dancing bubbles from escaping too soon.

How to serve wine:

White: Use a glass with tulip-shaped bowl and tall thin stem
Sparkling: Always serve sparkling wine in tall narrow flutes. Helps to keep those dancing bubbles from escaping too soon
Dessert: Use small glasses with unique shapes.

A wine glass should be filled 1/3 to ½ full. This is so the "bouquet" is released; the wonderful aroma that comes from swirling your glass of wine.

While wine is the adult beverage of choice with certain meals, wine with Asian meals can be a disaster. Rich heavier foods need rich heavier wines. Light foods should be served with light wines.

At one time people carried wine around in animal skins with the hairy side turned towards the inside and covered with pitch or they carried clay jars with handles. Of course, the skins were cleaned, but the hairy part doesn't sound too appealing. Bottles didn't come along until the 17th century which, when sealed with a cork, kept the bottle of the mouth-watering grape beverage able to be a stored for a long period of time.

Wine cellars should be dark, dry, well-ventilated, and maintain a temperature of 58 F. Fluctuating temperatures will be the enemy of your wine collection. Bottled wine should be stored on its side in bins or racks. Wine is stored on its side to keep the cork from shrinking and letting air into the bottle spoiling the wine.

Spritzer
1 cup dry white wine
½ cup club soda

Fill glass half full with broken ice. Pour wine over ice then add club soda. Spritzer can be enhanced with peach schnapps.

A cocktail umbrella actually serves a purpose. It keeps the ice from melting and the temperature of the drink at its ideal temperature.

Others Drinks and Drinks Men Should Never Order

Who doesn't like a Margarita? In the right place. It's a perfect complement to a festive bowl stuffed with salty chips accompanied by a tongue zapping salsa, but Margaritas have their place. You won't see your buddy sipping on one of those fruity drinks at the sports bar. Leave the fiesta drink where it belongs; back at El Diablos.

Umbrella Drinks or Ice Cream Drinks; those fruity, creamy concoctions can make an impression and probably not the impression you're looking for. First thought of a guy sipping on a little number full of cute little chunks of fruit skewered to an umbrella? Raised eyebrows? Move to the other side of the room? Looks delicious, order one for yourself? Leave these drinks to the college girls. Loose one guy card.

Everyone is familiar with the tasty little appetizer usually dressed up with an olive, strawberry, or umbrella. The cocktail can be traced back to the 19th century. The first cocktail to be created was the martini. It caught on quickly eventually morphing itself into the classic "dry martini" which became very popular. Cocktails also popped up during prohibition. The so-called "moonshine" which was being passed around was questionable both in taste and quality and the ingredients in the cocktail with their fruity or fizzy ingredients disguised the unrefined taste of homemade alcohol.

Cocktails often have quirky and unusual names. At one time, the delectable drink was named after famous people like Marilyn Monroe and Charlie Chaplain or famous places such as the Singapore Sling which was invented in a famous hotel in Singapore. There is even a cocktail named after Rob Roy, a novel written by Sir Walter Scott and, of course, the name of the beloved horse of the poet and duelist Andrew McClung who fancied himself a bit like the English poet, Sir Walter.

If you start the evening with a stiff cocktail such as a vodka drink on an empty stomach you'll get your buzz early which may help you to lose your appetite. Before you order that frothy, fruity little cocktail number on a date or consider trying an "appletini" while entertaining work clients, reflect on what your choice may suggest about your personality. Does your preference of a drink reveal something about you? Compliment your meal with the right drink.

A good drink for a business meeting would be a vodka (or wodka as my friend from Norway used to call it) and tonic, or gin and tonic. You do not have to order what your boss is drinking. People who drink Whisky/Scotch on the Rocks are people who usually have a few drinks a week. Most people who order martinis are experienced drinkers. Many are older, but if they are young, they tend to know their way around a liquor cabinet. A Manhattan is just as the name suggests. A mature man drink made of bourbon and vermouth.

As long as it is vodka or gin don't ever ask for the martini list. A woman does that. The only time to order a top shelf liquor in a juice base drink is when you plan on having a lot of them so your hangover won't be so bad.

Appletini, Chocotini, any Fruity/Sweety-Tini is a drink for the younger gals. It is a delightfully attractive alcoholic little number usually with the rim decorated with some peculiar addition like chocolate or graham cracker crumbs. Lose one guy card.

Rum and Coke, the old college standby. Rum and cola as a signature drink suggests familiarity and someone who is unlikely to try something new. People who drink rum and cola are comfortable with the familiar.

Bloody Mary, named after the former queen of England Mary I who earned her nickname burning heretics strapped to a post, are usually for older ladies who order these colorful numbers or folks who are trying to stave off a hangover.

Screwdriver: The drink for the man who doesn't want to taste the drink. Orange juice disguises the alcohol.

Cosmopolitan or Cosmo is a drink for the "barfly".

Does your choice of drink reveal something about you? Complement your meal with the right drink.

The last place in the body to be cleared of alcohol is the brain. So... that's why everyone looks so good after the bar closes.

The Drive to Succeed Comes in All Sizes

"This little fellow comes in, with a high voice, and says, "hi" remembered the owner of one restaurant in California. The fellow had, over the years, sold many things: coffee beans, paper cups, and even real estate. He first started in his Uncle's soda fountain engaging customers with his friendly smile and soon found out he could sell more than a soft drink.

One day while selling milk shake mixers to a restaurant he noticed the two brothers who ran the establishment had an impressive system called the Speede Service System, which enabled them to process the food quickly and get it out to their customers. Always the consummate salesman, he talked the owners into selling him a franchise even though they had turned down an offer from the Carnation Milk Company.

Although the place specialized in hamburgers, he once tried to sell a "hulaburger" and a pastry called the Kolacky to his customers. Both ideas failed. Ever the salesman, he was aware that it was not enough to provide good tasting food, he needed to be able to sell it so that no child could resist it. Yes, this franchise owner knew that every customer counted, even the littlest one. The food was wrapped in pretty packages, which included a toy. One time there were over 80 different types of Furbies to choose from and another time, many different Teenie Beanie babies included in the colorful package. The giveaway of the Beanie babies was one of the most successful advertising promotions ever in America. Adults would buy the food just to add one to *their* collection.

Willard Scott, the famous TV weatherman dressed up like a clown to promote the restaurant. Playgrounds were built and catchy commercial jingles sang the joy of how much fun it was to go to the food place. Its golden arches beckoned the little ones like the pied piper, but in this case, the cute customers also brought along their parents or grandparents to McDonalds. And the salesman with the high-pitched voice? Why, it was Ray Kroc, "Mr. McDonalds" himself owner extraordinaire and persistent pitchman who never forgot that all customers matter, even the littlest ones.

Bibliography

Beyer, Rick. The Greatest Stories Never Told. 100 Tales From History to Astonish, Bewilder, and Stupefy. Sywell: Igloo Books Ltd, 2007.

Botham, Noel. The Best Book of Useless Information Ever. New York, NY: Penguin Group, 2008.

Bly, Robert. Iron John Addison-Menlo Park, CA: Wesley Publishing Company, Inc. Reading, 1990.

Boyett ,Jason. A Guy's Guide to Life. How to become a man in 208 Pages or Less! Nashville, Tenn: W Publishing Group Thomas Nelson Inc.2004.

Cawthorne, Nigel. A History of Pirates. Blood and Thunder on the High Seas. London, England: Arcturus Publishing Limited, 2003.

Davidson. Lance S. Ludicrous Laws & Mindless Misdemeanors. New Jersey: Castle Books, 2004.

Eldredge, John. Wild at Heart. Nashville, Tenn: Thomas Nelson, Inc. 2001.

Fletcher, Connie. What Cops Know. Today's Police tell the inside story of their work on America's Streets. New York, NY: Simon and Schuster Inc, 1990.

Frankl, Viktor. Man's Search for Meaning. Boston, Mass: Beacon Press, 1959, 1962, 1984, 1992, 2006.

Frankl, Viktor. The Will to Meaning. Foundations and Applications of Logotherapy. New York, NY: Penguin Group,1969,1988.

Gladwell, Malcolm. The Tipping Point. How Little Things Can Make a Big Difference .New York, NY: Little, Brown, and Company, 2000.

Gladwell, Macolm. Blink. The Power of Thinking Without Thinking. Little, Brown, & Company. New York, Boston, London. 2005.

Hobbes, Nicholas. Essential Militaria. New York, NY: Grove Press, 2003.

Holland, Barbara. Gentleman's Blood- A History of Dueling. New York, NY: Bloomsbury Publishing. 2003.

Jackson, Michael. Great Beer Guide 500 Classic Brews. London, New York: Dorling Kindersley. 2000.

Joseph ,Robert and Rand, Margaret. K.I.S.S. Guide to Wine. London, New York : DK Publishing, 2000.

Lewis. Robert. Raising a Modern-Day Knight Wheaton, Illinois: Tyndale House Publishers,1997.

Luongo, Gerald, J. Surviving Federal Prison Camp. Chapel Hill, NC: Professional Press:.2004.

May, Larry. Strikwerda, Robert A. Editors. Rethinking Masculinity. Lanham, Maryland: Rowman & Little-field Publishers, 1992.

Mercer, Charles. Alexander the Great. American Heritage, Inc.1962, 2004.

Messner, Michael A. Power at Play, Sports and the Problem of Masculinty. Boston, Mass: Beacon Press Books, 1992.

Morely, Patrick. The Young Man in th Mirror. A Rite of Passage into Man-hood. Nashville, TN: Broadman & Holman Publishers. 2003

Morely, Patrick. The Seven Seasons of a Man's Life. Nashville, TN: Thomas Nelson, Inc., Publishers. 1995.

Campbell, Andrea. Making Crime Pay. The Writer's Guide to Criminal Law, Evidence, and Procedure.   New York, NY: Allworth Press:,2002.

Pickering, David. From Blackbeard to Walking the Plank Pirates. London, New York, Harper-Collins Publishers,2006.

Sharp. Clive. How to Survive Federal Prison Camp. A Guidebook for those caught up in the system. Port Townsend, WA, .Loompanics Unlimited, 1997.

Sheehy, Gail. Understanding Men's Passages. Discovering the New Map of Men's Lives. New York, NY: The Ballantine Publishing Group, 1998, 1999.

Internet Sources

"Wine Wise –How to Serve
Wine",http://www.oldandsold.com/articles22/wine-2.shtml March, 20,
2008.

Bad Fads Museum, http://www.badfads.com/pages/about.html,
February, 17,2008

Source: Prison and Jail Inmates at Midyear 2006, U.S. Bureau of Justice
Statistics.

http://www.wilderdom.com/intelligence/IQUnderstandingInterpreting.ht
ml

http://www.americaslibrary.gov/cgbin/page.cgi/jb/nation/hamburr_1Am
ericanrevolution.com/AlexanderHamiltonsDuel.htm

http://www.crazyfads.com/

http://www.prisonexp.org/

http://www.answers.com/topic/list-of-short-men

Elizabeth White, 1 IN 36 U.S. Residents Behind Bars By Elizabeth White
 The Associated

Press   Monday 22 May 2006 http://www.eyewitness
tohistory.com/duel.htm

Other books by B.J. Bradley:

 14.95 Paperback

 14.95 Paperback

 14.95 Paperback

 15.95 Paperback

 15.95 Paperback

www.ingramcontent.com/pod-product-compliance
Lightning Source LLC
Chambersburg PA
CBHW030016290326
41934CB00005B/355